I AM NOT A
SALESPERSON

SUCCEED IN SALES BY BEING YOU

SANA VASLI

Copyright © 2014 Sana Vasli

ISBN: 1500128414
ISBN-13: 978-1500128418

CONTENTS

1 INTRODUCTION

Working with yet another large sales- and service-oriented organisation, it dawned on me—people do not like to sell. It was amazing: I would meet people ranging from the most talented and high-performing salespeople, to those new to the arena of sales, and the feedback was always consistent. After digging deeper, they would confess their darkest secrets of how asking questions felt intrusive and closing sales was pushy. There is a world of *good guys* out there who are clouded by the perception that salespeople are evil. These individuals deny their profession through the use of euphemisms to describe their line of work at a family barbeque. They will call themselves *'associates'*, *'consultants'*, *'advisors'*, *'specialists'* and anything else that screams, "I am not a salesperson!"

For years I have been working with organisations at all stages of the sales culture continuum and have witnessed this notion of denial being most pronounced in companies that are either shifting from service to sales, are small companies that have a need to sell themselves or those who do not have a long history in sales. In these organisations people who work in back office are honest, steady and reliable (i.e. the *good guys*) and people in sales are cut-throat, shift and dishonest (i.e. the *bad guys*). Is this true? Do companies proactively seek out bad people to join their organisation and ask them to create the first impression of their brand? Unlikely! So why do people feel this way?

Of course a large part of the development of this perception comes from film and television that represent salespeople as cheesy, cunning, pushy and manipulative. Then, when you witness the smallest glimmering of these behaviours in an actual salesperson, that initial perception converts to a reality. On the other hand, when you see a warm, kind and caring salesperson, you of course do not associate him or her with sales and you think, 'Wow, wasn't she a lovely person? Such great service!' Another area that has turned good people away from developing the skills of sales are traditional sales training courses and books—yes, books! This will be explored in more depth later; however, sales training material are often filled with 'how to be a top-gun salesperson', 'get rich from commission', 'reach the top' and 'influence strangers'. All of these catchphrases and gimmicks are focused on profiting oneself, which is not always a motivator for the *good guys*. For those who take pride in providing a service, you would be more interested in a course that focused on meeting the needs of our customers—right? So, where are the courses entitled, 'How to meet your customers' needs', 'Delight your customers through sales', 'Sales strategies for genuine caring people'? There is certainly a market for these people, so why no courses and books?

This was a question I was faced with when coaching a retail banking executive on sales. The question got me curious and I responded with, "Nate, I don't know why," to which he replied, "Maybe you should write one." This book represents my contribution back to the sales industry that has given me so much.

I Am Not a Salesperson takes a backwards approach to traditional sales training and starts from the customer's perspective, then moves to techniques and best practice. This approach is balanced between how the salesperson should act and how the customer responds. The content within the following pages is a mixture of self-developed ideas/concepts, experiences, observing the best of the best, the study of behavioural sciences and a lot of great research developed in literature before this book. I am a lover of reading and have used some of the gems I have found in hundreds of books I have read, and where relevant have given credit to the original authors. As sales knowledge is born in action, some concepts that are addressed here as original work may have been written about before. If this is true and the original author has not been sourced, that is not intentional; please get in contact with me and I will happily correct it.

This book will discuss the distinct processes that take place within a sales conversation and how an authentic and caring person can use their natural behaviours to shine in sales while maintaining their values and integrity without turning into the villain. This book will help you leverage your strengths rather than focusing on the gaps between your current skills and those of traditional salespeople.

This text is not a set of isolated theories nor is it designed to be read passively and understood philosophically. Remember, like all effective learning approaches, this content will only be effective if it is embedded in action. This book is based on practice and therefore should be used in practice.

There is a lot to be gained for those who wish to succeed without losing themselves in performing uncomfortable, unnatural and non-authentic behaviours.

2 I AM NOT A SALESPERSON

WHY SHOULD I READ THIS BOOK?

The idea for this book originated from a topic that is growing day by day in it's relevance. When we look around us, the customer service industry (in its literal sense) is dying away and an emerging cut-throat sales society is taking shape in its place. Every commercial business, charity organisation, blue-collar/white-collar worker, medical service, government department and individual employee is out there trying to swim through the bloody sea of competition and sell their products like never before. Deals are becoming aggressive, prices are being forced downwards and we are seeing an increase in desperate tactics to capture customers.

So what if you don't like to sell?

This shift from service to sales is affecting everyone involved; business owners, sales managers, customers and customer service representatives. I, too, have not been immune to the impacts of our changing environment. With regard to selling, I have experienced just about everything, from owning a small door-to-door sales business to senior retail management, to consulting with major banks in Australia on sales strategy and business transformation. I have met a variety of people along the way and have witnessed some common trends that are not being addressed effectively. Put simply, we are in denial about the shift from service to sales and the impact this is having on people who are not natural-born ~~killers~~ salespeople. Of course, every industry has its own unique challenges; however, one thing I have consistently observed through a variety of industries is a lack of content in sales training targeted to those who do not consider themselves salespeople. Organisations have adopted one of two extremes—high-intensity, outcome-focused sales training on the one hand or taking short cuts by adopting a *monkey see, monkey do* training environment on the other. The latter has always puzzled me. I have always wondered what type of organisation would rely on the unmonitored behaviour and potential bad habits of their staff to educate their up-and-coming sales force.

Those who choose to conduct intense sales training that employs bold and seemingly aggressive tactics, can be intimidating to many and unsuitable to people's perceptions of how we should view our customers. Imagine an individual who loves their customers and cares for their well-being, and hears the war cry of an overly enthusiastic sales trainer screaming, "Let's smash in some sales!" Telling someone who does not like to sell, 'This training will turn you into a top-gun salesperson,' is also not going to excite them into behavioural change, it will in fact achieve the opposite. For many people, a salesperson is the last thing they want to become. Think about it. When we were children we dreamed of being famous, like a pop singer or an astronaut; I can't recall anyone telling me they dreamt of being an insurance salesperson.

In recent times, I witnessed a training session where a sales coach was talking to a financial planner, Diane, whose job was to sell her services and expertise to customers in order for them to increase their financial wealth. In this session, the coach looks at Diane and says, "By the time we are finished here, you are going to double your commissions," to which she responded, "Double my commissions? I am here to give customers what they want—not sell things. Selling is not for me." "Excuse me?" replied the confused coach. "So how else do you suppose to make a living as a financial planner?" Diane looked at her coach blankly and to all of us it became very obvious that doubling commissions or becoming a sales hero was not going to be a motivator in this situation. As you may have already guessed, the session didn't end very well, and three months later I heard that Diane had started a hairdressing course to get away from selling.

Diane felt like she was making the right move; however, the reality is that we all require sales skills in one way or another. The sad part is Diane had great capability; however, the difference between Diane and other financial planners is that she chose to adopt negative perceptions about salespeople and the word *sales*, which stifled her success. The irony of Diane's story is that she escaped one sales profession only to seek refuge in another. Diane, if you are reading this, I'm sure you have figured out by now that hairdressers are also salespeople. So, the first piece of knowledge that Diane and everyone else who has felt her pain needs to know is that the ability to influence others and communicate effectively is not a set of exclusive skills of a salesperson; rather, they are life skills. Parents, teachers, friends, husbands, wives, children, mechanics, taxi drivers, dentists and IT programmers are all salespeople. They all need to know the skills of selling—without needing to compromise their integrity or employ a set of behaviours that salespeople are stereotyped with today.

WHO SHOULD BE READING THIS?

This book has been written for all the good guys out there who are working in the field of sales but who don't necessarily connect with the broad perception of a salesperson. The first group are those at the forefront—people in sales roles that don't see themselves as a tradition salesperson. If you identify with this category, you are being told that your job (which you may have viewed as helping people), has targets and KPIs that, if unmet, can result in uncomfortable performance-management conversations. This book will hopefully relieve a lot of that stress, allowing you to succeed without turning you into something you are not and don't want to be. This book will share with you some simple ways for meeting these targets and winning the game of sales, without selling your soul and turning off your customers. You will not read about out-dated methods like ABC (Always Be Closing) and Feel, Felt, Found ("I understand how you feel"). You will be able to adapt these principles and examples into your own language that customers like to hear, and continue to create satisfied buyers.

Customer service managers and sales leaders are also relevant readers of this book. You might be the sales manager of a computer company selling to corporate clients, the head waiter of a restaurant, a bank manager or a small-business owner—either way, the contents within this single volume will be useful and relevant in coaching your teams to success. This book will not only help you improve the sales capability of your staff, but also demonstrate how to break down the walls of sales resistance and motivate your sales team by tapping into their values.

If you are a professional salesperson who loves to sell and wants to add more tips to your tool belt, then you will also get a lot out of this book. *I Am Not A Salesperson*, will increase your passion about customer-focused selling, while giving a fresh perspective on your industry.

Lastly, if you are someone who is interested in convincing customers to do whatever you want, against their will, and care more about commissions than the customers' well-being, then you *NEED* this book. You may not like the contents, but for the sake of your customers and your future success, please don't put this down!

…BUT I AM NOT A SALESPERSON

Many training programs and sales books are aimed at the eager salesperson who is inspired by targets and thrives on competition. Authors are often writing for a target audience who already see themselves as salespeople and want to build on that persona. The people that we often forget about are those that need the most help—people that must sell, when they don't want to. Many of us joined companies or started businesses not taking into account the requirement to sell. Whether customer facing or not, most roles require the ability to sell and it is increasingly becoming a skill for survival.

So what happens if you don't see yourself as a salesperson? Before we address this, let's explore the concept of '*I am not a salesperson*' as this is a phrase that I hear frequently in both my profession and day-to-day conversations with people.

If that phrase resonates with you, then let me ask you: Why are you not a salesperson? Is it because you do not have the capacity to acquire the skills of being a salesperson? Unlikely! Is it because you were not endowed with the sales gene at birth? I don't think so. On the other hand, is it because you look at the salespeople you know in life and see in films and do not connect with their behaviours? Perhaps. Whenever I ask people, the most common answer is, "Selling is just not me." 'Not *me*' you say? What does it really mean for something to be not you? As humans, are we limited to a certain number of things that we can and cannot be? Are we all born with a preordained list of things that we are comfortable with and everything that lives outside these boundaries are *not me*?

To break this phrase down and bust some myths, we can use an example of something else that you may consider *not you*. *Not you* could include anything from wearing a particular style of clothing that you don't like, listening to an unfavourable genre of music, going bungee jumping, eating a particular vegetable, or public speaking. We tend to associate certain behaviours that align with our perception of our identities. For example, A, B and C are acceptable actions that are congruent with our identity, and actions X, Y and Z are not within those bounds.

For the sake of simplicity, let's use the example of Trent, a seminar participant, who boldly stated, "I hate the opera, it's just not me." Trent had made a cognitive decision that viewing the opera stepped outside of his bounds of 'normal' and did not line up with his perception of himself. After Trent stated that the opera was *not him*, I followed this by asking him, "So if going to the opera is not you and I forced you to watch Madame Butterfly... who would you become?" Trent, with a puzzled look on his face, answered, "Uh, I'd still be me, right?" Exactly. Your identity is not going to suddenly change the moment you watched someone sing on stage or eat sushi or speak in front of a crowd for the first time. You are still you, only now with a new set of behaviours, an added experience or new life skills. Trent's visits to the Opera do not take anything away from his identity—in fact it only expands it. Trent is now himself, plus more.

This type of discomfort that Trent experiences is what we will describe here as *learning*. Learning, or trying anything for the first time, is initially uncomfortable until it is performed enough times to become normal. The same principle applies to the phrase *'I am not a salesperson'*. Ask yourself the question: if you sold something through a compelling conversation with a customer, who do you suddenly become if this is *not you?* Are you now a product flogger who does not care about customers? Are you a sales-hungry animal? Are you a manipulative person without a conscious? Not a chance. Sales is not a way of life, a religion or a personality type. It's just a job! Being successful in sales simply requires you to adopt a set of behaviours and not to change a single part of who you are. As we have already demonstrated with Trent and the opera, you can change your behaviours and still be you. Therefore, when you sell, you are still *you* plus a new set of capabilities and actions.

There may be techniques you learn and practise from this book that you have never experienced before. This will be uncomfortable, which is a great indicator that you're learning something—congratulations. We have to always remember that learning something new or adopting a new behaviour does not suddenly seize our previous abilities to do something. It is not as if our minds are limited to a certain amount of disk space and new items bump out the old ones. Learning some simple tips around customer-focused selling will not take away your personality, your care for customers or your current capabilities. Instead, it will actually do the opposite: it adds more options for achieving the same desired outcomes. Learning is about adding choice, not taking it away! For those of you who think, "I am not a salesperson", remember, by selling you become more of *you* and not less.

WHAT I WILL LEARN AND WHY IT IS IMPORTANT

As mentioned earlier, sales skills are life skills. Think about the broad and general soft skills acquired in sales. You learn communications skills, interpersonal skills, questioning techniques, body language and the ability to take control of your attitude. Couldn't all of those skills apply to any job? There are also many life roles that these skills apply to. All in all, learning about the art of sales is essentially mastering the art of conversations—and, let's face it, conversations are an important art to master.

How many proper conversations would you have every day? 20… 30? Depending on your profession, over 100? So we know that conversations are frequent, so let's explore how important they are. Let's imagine that you were having a perfectly normal day at work and then all of a sudden you had a really negative conversation with your manager or colleague—would this impact the mood of your day? What if you had a week or month full of bad conversations? Would that not damage the quality of your week/month? What if you endured a lifetime of negative and deflating conversations? Would this impact the quality and enjoyment of your life? Of course it would. Therefore, our happiness in life is dependent on the quality of our conversations (among other things of course). Conversations play a big role in our lives, so we need to get this right. What if the conversations we were initiating with customers, family and colleagues were always negative ones and we didn't know it? It's time to master this art.

Other key insights that you can take away from this book are adopting the right mindset, building genuine connections with our customers, staying interesting and relevant in sales, helping customers make decisions through asking great questions, being compelling in delivering recommendations, responding to objections in a professional and caring way, closing the sale without being pushy, and providing sales management tools for current and aspiring leaders.

GETTING THE MOST OUT OF THIS BOOK

This book is not a set of theories that make you ponder; it should serve you as a body of knowledge that can immediately be translated into action. To get maximum effectiveness from this book, you should be continuously applying these principles and tips as you read through it.

If it helps, keep a notepad by your side to write down the things that you will use immediately and include details around how to specifically apply this to your reality. Allow this book to be your pocket coach and let it follow you to successfully combating some of the challenges you face.

OUR CHANGING WORLD

In the early '90s, our world was very different to what it is today. We did not have readily available access to information, people used to only buy from bricks-and-mortar retailers, music was on cassette tapes, and petrol was certainly not seen as a luxury item.

Our world was very simple, particularly in terms of the relationship between the consumer and the merchant.

This relationship was simple in nature. The customer had a need and the merchant fulfilled it. Think back (if you're old enough) to the early '90s and imagine that you were to walk into a retail bank, for example. Your experience would be dramatically different to what it is today. You would have walked into a sterile, overly air-conditioned branch, met process-driven workers and seen bland-coloured walls. You may have filled in a deposit slip, joined the queue, walked over to the counter, told the bank representative what you wanted—and guess what? You got it! No questions asked—it was that simple!

Now, only a couple of decades later, imagine that you are walking into that same bank. As you approach the automatic doors, your optical lobe, the part of the brain that controls vision, is being bombarded with an overkill of promotional posters, balloons and streamers telling you what the latest and greatest offer is and why you need it now. As you walk through the door, you are then caught off guard by a well-dressed, slick-haired, highly perfumed 'greeter' who is excited to have a conversation with you. What you innocently assumed to be a friendly discussion about your long-term goals to buy a house was in fact a highly profitable lead-generation activity for the staff member to hand you over to some type of 'specialist' who, for the sake of simplicity, we can refer to as a salesperson. You then walk over to the teller and ask to deposit some money. As the teller is processing your transaction, he/she is holding onto your card with a firm grip, to anchor you in. You can't go anywhere—it's a trap! They keep you in front of them for as long as they can, so you can hear about the great offer they have on their new low-rate credit card. You repeatedly decline the offer and desperately try to leave. As you power-walk out of the door, that slick-haired greeter blocks your path and hands over a pile of brochures with business cards stapled to the front. You look at them with confusion, to which they cunningly respond, "Our home loan specialist will call you within twenty-four hours," to which you reply, "...but I didn't give you my number." The greeter now looks you back in the eye and says, "We already have your number on file."

This type of sales practice has been rampant in the banking industry for the last few years. I can recall an article that was written in news.com about the amount of pressure and focus that the four major banks in Australia were applying to double—and in some cases triple—their sales. This resulted in significant action that led to a major revolt by the Financial Services Union for a number of the banks.

This cultural shift from reactive and submissive customer service to proactive selling is certainly not limited to the banking industry. For a number of years now this shift has taken place in industries in which the average consumer would least expect it. In the past few years we have seen newsagents, mechanics, apprentice carpenters, restaurant waiters, charities, schools, universities and even churches make the shift from service to sales. Think about your workplace: are there any staff members who are being asked to sell more than before? Are we asking people to find a sales opportunity in every customer interaction? Perhaps it has been you who has been told that your role has changed and that just *being nice* to customers does not cut it anymore. You are told to think and act like a salesperson. You may have started to notice a new breed of salesy-like staff joining your organisation and topping the leader board. You may be the owner of a small business in a highly competitive market and needing to become your own sales team.

On the other hand, if you are a manager leading a team, department or organisation through this cultural shift, you may have loyal veteran employees telling you, "This was not what I signed up to do," or, "I find it disrespectful to sell to my regular customers," and most commonly, "I am not a salesperson—it's just not me."

Whatever happened to those safe environments where we could avoid the cheesy used-car salesman and hounding real estate agents? What happened to our world that is driving our customer-focused fulfilment channels to shift into sales-hungry industries? Why the shift?

WHY THE SHIFT?

Without delving too deeply into the nitty-gritty of the past, present and future financial crises, which is a topic that this author is by no means an expert in, it is safe to say that our financial world has been unstable. Post-global financial crisis, consumers have been under pressure and consequently our businesses are feeling it.

Whether or not this drop in consumer confidence has developed from an educated and well-informed understanding, is not an overwhelming concern. What is important to know is that it is real and this strain on the market doesn't look like it's going anywhere anytime soon.

The consequent drop in consumer confidence and loss in sales has caused organisations to react by continuing to push harder. What else were they to do? We cannot simply expect all organisations to enter into an expensive price war in the hope of winning market share, nor can many companies afford to increase their sales force. The organisations that we work for are stuck, backed into a corner with no options other than to do what any of us would do: adapt. These organisations looked at the resources around them and asked themselves which staff members were close enough to customers to bring in more sales and which ones would help them reduce costs. In other words, who will provide more income to the business and who is more of an expense that we can cut? Look on the bright side: if your organisation is asking you to sell, that makes you one of the lucky ones who kept their job.

SERVICE IS STILL IMPORTANT

If your organisation is making the shift from service to sales or you have entered a role that requires you to sell, you will notice that there will be a heavy emphasis on selling and sales behaviours/skills. This does not mean that service is not important. In fact, according to research conducted by Bluewolf, 59% of customers will switch brands to get better service and 73% will spend more money if a company has a good service history. This cultural shift towards sales should not be mistaken for a complete switch off from service by moving sales in its place. It is very common for people who embrace the change early and wish to become ambassadors of sales to move from one end of the spectrum to the other. This is evident in one of the major banks in Australia, which had a number of customer complaints posted on their various social network pages regarding the over-the-top enthusiasm of sales staff being too pushy. This was a shock for customers as it was vastly different to the bank's previous behaviour.

Once this happens, management will naturally swing the pendulum in the other direction and conduct training on providing outstanding customer service. As a consequence of this reactive move, sales drop and then the focus is back on selling—and the cycle continues. We need to learn how to balance the two as one cannot exist without the other.

Sales without service will lead to poor customer experience and eventually viral word of mouth and disengagement from clients. Service in the absence of sales will be nice for our reputation; however, it will not yield any benefits for the customer or the organisation and is unsustainable for the company's future. Sales and service can coexist and we should avoid creating dichotomies between the arenas of sales and service. Sustainable success is dependent on the integration of sales and service as one act. This concept is best described by Henry Ford when he said, "If you find out what men want and give them that, you are pleasing them. If you find out what is good for them and give them that, you are performing a service."

Competition is becoming increasingly aggressive, and your ability to win customers' loyalty will hinge on your capacity to demonstrate the value that your products deliver and the service that they receive throughout the lifecycle of purchasing your products. So when is the best time to deliver outstanding value to our customers? Answer: before someone else does. So there is no time to lose.

WHERE DO SALESPEOPLE COME FROM?

If we think back hard enough, I'm sure we can all remember a time where salespeople used to fit into the organisation. They were that obscure department of overly enthusiastic, cheesy egomaniacs that boasted about their commission and used their hands a lot in conversations. Salespeople were the cut-throat, fearless, bold and money-centred humans of our society. If we do not necessarily possess all of the above characteristics, then why are we being asked to sell? Times have clearly changed.

Becoming a salesperson is traditionally not a lifelong ambition for many people. As briefly mentioned before, at a young age, people want to be astronauts, doctors, lawyers and celebrities—or in my case a garbage man. You fall into sales in some way or another. It is rarely apart of the big plan. In many cases, becoming a salesperson is an accident—in the same way it has now happened to you!

SALES AS A DIRTY BUSINESS

In many organisations, sales has become a dirty word. It is a word that makes most people cringe at the best of times. Many people who work in management, admin, back office and operational roles will sometimes do anything to avoid being associated with selling. I remember working with an organisation whose managers would use sales as a punishment. If anyone misbehaved or came to work late, they would be summoned to an evening with the door-to-door sales team or spend an hour with the outbound call centre. This form of punishment became so popular that it had its own title of 'prison time'. It is no wonder people shiver and shriek when we are told to sell. For years we have continued to breed this perception of salespeople and now it has come back to bite us, as we are being asked to join them.

I have spent many years working with organisations that are making this shift. One would be amazed to see what industries and roles are actually making the shift. What would you say if I told you that pharmacies, mechanics and some plumbers have sales targets? How interesting is it to think that a health professional like a pharmacist is proactively selling? What next, the heart surgeon who throws in a discount limb amputation with every triple bypass? And I don't know what I am more afraid of; the hustling pharmacist pushing drugs down my throat, or the commission-hungry roadside mechanic? Every industry that deals with some type of client is vulnerable to the shift.

The industries mentioned above that are making the shift consist of professionals whom we have no choice but to trust. They have unique skills or knowledge that we rely on. Recently, I was at a pharmacy at the airport asking for a remedy for my ears popping due to the air pressure of the airplane—*don't judge me*. What I expected to be a straightforward conversation turned into a product-flogging event by the pharmacist. As she was recommending the earplugs, I found her looking me up, down, left and right to identify triggers to cross-sell me to other product groups. She heard the slightest sniffle in my nose and told me that I needed a particular nasal spray to clear my nose, which would make me more comfortable on my flight. The pharmacist then introduced me to her assistant who timidly tried to take me through other products that would make my flight more enjoyable—everything from neck pillows to Sudoku puzzles.

Now, don't get me wrong; both the pharmacist and her assistant were probably telling the truth about everything they were recommending. In fact, those things most probably would have benefitted me. So why did it not work? What were the elements that turned me off as a customer? What was happening behind the scenes that made the assistant so nervous to introduce new products to me? Why was it so hard?

As fascinating as it was to see a health professional make this shift, it did not need to be so hard. Sales is not that complicated. There are some really simple steps that can make both the customer and the salesperson equally as comfortable.

THE UTILITY VIEW

Industries that are making the shift towards a sales focus are often suffering from what is referred to as the *utility view*. The utility view is the mindset that consumers have of an organisation and the belief that their primary function is to provide a service or utility that people need and not necessarily want. If your organisation is viewed as a utility, consumers often believe that you are not entitled to make excessive profits as this is manipulative of people's needs. This may be because your industry was founded as a service-providing utility and core part of the organisation of a community.

At the inception of retail banking, the bank manager was seen as a highly respected and esteemed member of society and banks were established in towns and villages to protect people and help them in times of need. This view makes it challenging for organisations to start proactively selling in order to maintain their growth and longevity in this competitive market. This is one of the reasons there is so much contention when a bank CEO's salary increase is announced. Consumers with this view cannot stomach the idea of your organisation making profit through charging fees, hence the pushback on proactive selling. Many insurance organisations are still considered not-for-profit and continually attempt to convince their customers and employees that profits are not their aim. How long can this last for?

This view needs to shift in order for organisations to progress; however it will not shift overnight through clever marketing or redesigning retail outlets. The shift begins with our mindset. Two years ago, I was walking through the call centre of a major insurance company and a customer service representative was having an argument with their manager over their current sales performance. The sales agent was throwing out every excuse as to why they were unable to sell, despite the fact that his peers were meeting their targets. As the tension escalated, the sales agent reached a new peak in his arguments, saying, "I can't believe this! You want me to sell more policies so we can make a profit, don't you?" His team leader was shocked and, in a knee-jerk fashion, responded with, "No no, I'm not."

Hold the phone. Why do we shy away from this reality? Your job is to make a profit! The longer that we live in denial about the nature of our organisation and the roles we play, the longer the shift will drag out and success will not be reached. There is nothing wrong, unethical or sinister about being successful or making money. Of course, I am not suggesting that this be the primary aim of every activity, but it is one of the necessary outcomes of every company, just like customer satisfaction, brand awareness and engaged employees. More often than not, sales agents say things like, "We're only trying to make profit" for one or two reasons: it's either a sense of shame in being in the sales profession or an excuse not to be proactive as this requires more effort than being reactive.

If it is the former, then we need to rise above this and protect our mindset. Let's not allow public perceptions and myths guide our careers.

3 THE SALES MINDSET

MAYBE WE GOT IT WRONG

In my line of work, I have had the pleasure of sitting through many sales training seminars. The organisations I have worked with have varied in their degrees of sales maturity. Some companies are developing highly experienced and accomplished sales professionals, while others are training inductees who have never sold a thing in their lives. In these sessions, the facilitator will often set the stage to gauge the level of sales knowledge among the participants. They often begin with a question such as, "What is a salesperson?" or, "What do salespeople do?"

This question usually results in similar answers. One keen participant will positively respond with, "They educate, they help customers, they understand customer needs, they are the heroes of the universe". These are generally the answers people give when they are trying to impress the facilitator or manager. The vast majority of people stay quiet towards the beginning, until one courageous participant starts the rant on all of the negative things that salespeople can do. Traditionally, this list is a lot longer, as they rattle off comments such as, "Salespeople can be pushy... arrogant... in your face... they lie... they cheat... Salespeople only care about themselves and getting the sale."

How fascinating? On the one hand, salespeople are saintly and wish to help our customers and at the same time they are scamming con artists? Can a salesperson be both the hero and the villain?

Yes. Salespeople are capable of both good and bad practices, so we need to stop asking what a salesperson does and who they are. Rather, we need to concentrate on what are the elements of a successful salesperson? Successful in getting results as well as being fulfilled emotionally, intellectually and financially. Think about this question through the lens of a customer. What do you like to hear when you are buying? What excites you into a buying mode? What do you need to know before making a decision?

Imagine you were to go and buy a car from a dealership and you are faced with a number of different salespeople. Who will you buy from? The first salesperson is pushy, cunning, quick with their words, not thorough, self-centred, in-your-face and all about the commission. Is that salesperson, who is persistently trying to close the deal, going to be successful in creating a satisfied buyer out of you? Of course not! So then why does everyone who thinks they will not be good at sales use reasoning like, "I'm not pushy enough," "I don't like making decisions for people and telling them what to do," "I care too much about my customers and don't want to lie to them?" These may be the qualities of many salespeople; however, we have just demonstrated that these are certainly not what it takes to be a successful one. This is the first myth to bust about sales success.

So, let's play the scenario once again, only with a different type of salesperson this time. You've walked into the car dealership and to your surprise you meet an approachable, neat and well-mannered individual who is kind, genuinely cares about your needs, attentively listens to you, honest about the car's suitability to your needs, gives you ample time to think and promised to helpful after the purchase. How would you have responded to this salesperson? You may not even have perceived their actions as selling, because they created a space for you to buy rather than roping you in with cheap hooks and corny one-liners to get you excited.

So maybe the world has got it wrong about salespeople and there's no doubt as to why: we remember the negative experiences with salespeople far more than the positive. This perception has a lasting effect and when we meet a *good* salesperson, we may not recognise them as sellers at all.

THE NOBILITY OF SELLING

Why are so many people ashamed of the profession of selling? Have bad people who joined the industry really ruined it for the rest of us? We cannot let this continue because the profession of selling is a noble one. If selling is so bad and manipulative, then why don't we make it illegal? What would be the implications?

If we were to remove salespeople from the world, many businesses could no longer afford to operate and consequently people would lose their jobs, unemployment would increase, taxes would go up to fund employment, and we probably wouldn't own half of the things in our house. Selling is what funds businesses and is critical to the upkeep of a healthy economy. We should be proud to work in such a profession and not just see it as a temporary job. Many great entrepreneurs and senior executives are where they are today because of their sales skills. How on earth would Steve Jobs, the co-founder of Apple, have gotten his business off the ground if he couldn't sell? Would Ghandi have had such a great following without being able to sell?

We need to be advocates and defenders of the noble profession in which we work.

STABILITY OF A SALES CAREER

Selling is a unique profession that allows you to take charge of your financial destiny. Your income is dependent on your skills and efforts to persevere. This type of mindset separates top and bottom performers. Many people exit the profession of sales due to its perceived instability—but is it the job that is unstable or is it the salesperson?

One can argue that they work in a volatile market and that there are 'ups and downs'. Some blame poor sales results on terrible managers, a bad team and ineffective training. Attitudes of blaming have been established from a young age, where we blamed teachers for poor maths skills, and later blamed partners for poor relationships.

Whether any of these reasons are true is not important. What is important is that salespeople need to take responsibility for their results and not let other people and their environment take control of their destiny.

To help bust this myth about instability, let me ask; is there someone in the industry who consistently achieves strong results? Maybe there are behaviours that we can perform on a regular basis that do not allow us to fall victim to changing markets and other industry trends.

The best salespeople keep their minds in focus and their activities consistent. They do not prospect when sales are low—they prospect all year round. Equally, they do not relax when sales are high.

Salespeople that demonstrate consistent success, never stop learning. Remember, you are the manager of your own training department and should always be thinking about the next area of development. If the company that you work for is not able to pay for your continuous education, then you should spend the money. Don't look at your education as a cost; look at it as the best investment that you can ever make. Even if you only learn one new technique from a training course, your money would have been well spent. It is often one or two techniques that stand between our present state and greater success.

An effective sales mindset requires us to take control of our destiny, write our own paycheque and determine how stable we wish to make our careers. Don't settle for instability—you deserve more.

SELLING SOMETHING THEY DON'T WANT

Undertaking the process of a sale can feel very selfish at times. It may seem that it is a process in which one party is convincing another to do something that they did not originally want to do. Salespeople, no matter how good they are, are not endowed with the abilities to control our minds and force us to go against our own will. So we need to remove these notions of selling out of our minds, as they are not true. As a customer there are certain things that you definitely would not purchase and other things that are within your scope of consideration. Take me for example; I have never had any alcohol in my life for religious, health and lifestyle reasons (which all three rank as high values). In the past 10 years I have clocked an extremely high amount of interstate flights and every time I walk through the airport I am called out by a couple of salespeople from the Wine Selectors kiosk, who sell subscriptions to an ongoing delivery of wine. To date, there has been no clever line, benefit statement or attempt at rapport building that has influenced me to stop and have a conversation about wine. Even if this store was manned by Zig Ziglar himself (a renowned sales master), I cannot imagine being influenced to buy.

To put this theory to the test, I once stopped over at a Wine Selectors kiosk with a colleague of mine as he loves wine and like me, loves the odd mystery-shop. The salesperson there mistakenly targeting me and ran me through a long list of the features and benefits of their variety of different wines. After telling her that I don't drink, she persisted by telling me how good it feels to be tipsy and it helps "loosen you up"—whatever that means! She continued to persist and of course nothing she could say led me to temptation. Salespeople may be trained in identifying unknown needs, however they are certainly not hired to force people against their own will. So we should never be afraid that what we do in sales is about convincing someone to do something what they don't want to do.

In recent years, neuroscientists have teamed up with marketing experts around the world to understand what it takes to make people buy. They are eagerly testing what colours are more powerful, which words pack the most punch, how impactful celebrity endorsements are, the effect that words popping up on the screen have or which combination of the above successfully pushes the *buying button*. Unfortunately for them, no such *buying button* has been discovered and there is no magic formula to getting a customer to do whatever you want them to do—unless you use hypnosis! Not even by scientifically understanding the human brain and what triggers it into behaviours can we forcibly sell a product or service to a customer. So never fear that by selling, you are doing the wrong thing and forcing customers into decisions. In general, customers are not completely gullible and we are not magicians or hypnotists—we are just having conversations.

Ensuring effective and sustainable sales conversations that our customers enjoy, is about creating a space and environment in which they feel comfortable to buy. As customers, we don't always enjoy being sold to—so why would our own clients feel different? Despite not liking being sold to, we do enjoy buying. So the more we help our customers buy, the more successful we will have.

HELPING PEOPLE THROUGH SALES

Most of the people I speak with who have struggled with making the shift from service to sales are plagued with this sense of guilt. They see proactive sales as an evil thing, and I repeatedly hear phrases like, "I feel bad selling stuff to people," "Asking questions about their needs is so intrusive," and, most of all, "I don't want to sell; I just like helping people." This can be seen as a praiseworthy and commendable mindset and one that many would encourage. The danger with this mindset, however, is that it is more often than not just an excuse not to sell and avoid the uncomfortable work.

Proactive selling is all about identifying customer needs, often in areas in which clients are not necessarily experts in; for example, real estate agents knowing the housing market or computer salespeople discussing the ins-and-outs of personal computing. Let's take a non-sales example; if you approached your doctor with regard to a flu virus and she identified that you also have a skin infection, should she ask you questions about it or is this too intrusive? Is she allowed to recommend a remedy to your unknown and unstated need? Of course she is. So, if it is okay for the doctor to do it, then why is it so different for the salesperson? Ask yourself: do you sell a product or service that helps people? The extent to which our products help customers may not be as obvious as that of the doctor; however, I am sure you can think of the benefits.

Imagine that you are now standing in front of your customer and you have identified an opportunity to help them. Do you just leave it to them to figure it out or do you start asking questions to uncover the prospect's need in order to create interest? Is this *helping them* or *selling*? Actually, it's both and this is what good salespeople do—they know the balance and they know where to draw the line. If you worked in a call centre for an insurance company, for example, and spoke with a person who asked only for third-party car insurance with an expensive car, would you ask them about a more comprehensive insurance? Is it not your duty of care to ensure that the customer is aware of the benefits available to them?

Looking back throughout history, we can see some of the most heroic salespeople—like Mother Teresa, for example, who successfully sold the idea of dedicating your life to the poor and sick; and Martin Luther King Jr. who is known for one of the most compelling sales presentations in history that started with, "I have a dream..."

The concept of helping customers does not only apply to heroic deeds and situations of crisis that a doctor or an aid worker deals with. What if you work in a clothes store and someone is trying on a pair of jeans that match a shirt you have in the store? As someone in the retail fashion industry, is it not also your duty of care to help the customer? So why do some people feel this sense of guilt? It's all in our heads! Remove it, be helpful, have great conversations and your customers will appreciate it! Identifying needs and proactively selling is *helping* and if it isn't, the customer will not buy. Let their actions be your feedback rather than any negative self-talk.

IT'S ALL ABOUT THE CUSTOMER... OR IS IT?

When working in sales, what motivates you? Traditional salespeople will tell you it is all about the commission/bonus and the recognition amongst management, peers and friends. People who are not your traditional salespeople, on the other hand, will tell you it is all about customer satisfaction and helping people. Is either right or wrong? No—however, extreme views on commission and an over-cautiousness on satisfaction can potentially lead to a lack of success in sales.

In terms of the way we approach the sales conversation, a customer centric view will lead to a successful and sustainable sales career. However, it must be noted that this view is not at variance with an expectation of financial reward. Just because we love our customers it does not mean that sales commissions are bad and that we should eschew financial rewards.

In the guise of being customer-focused, salespeople often say, "I don't care about the money/commission." It is no surprise that these same salespeople are rarely at the top of the sales leader board and also have the least-engaged customers. Their customers may not have a bad thing to say about them; however, if we were to ask them how this salesperson has effectively improved their current position, we may draw blank responses.

I for one do not believe salespeople who say, "I don't care about money." To see if this is true, we need to test the strength of this conviction by taking it to the extreme. If I was to tell this same person, who is on an average salary that their earning potential will increase by $100,000 for every sale, do you think that they would not care about money? So, it is very easy for someone who is not engaged in proactive selling to say that they are not motivated by the money, because it is not there. The point here is not to encourage people to be focused only on money, but to understand that it is OKAY to be rewarded for your work.

If you are a great customer-centric, value-based salesperson, then your commission and bonuses should be seen purely as a measurement of your ability to help others. The more commission you receive, the more people you have helped and provided benefits to. The less sales success you have had, the more customer needs you have neglected due to a false sense of customer care. This is a matter of mindset and not a question of ethics.

WHEN TIMES GET TOUGH

Anyone who has worked in sales can relate to tough times. Whether it be for a day, a week or even a month. Tough times can be caused by a variety of reasons, for example, the market may be down; new regulations may have been introduced; customers are not visiting your store; a new competitor is stealing our clients; targets have gone up; we have less staff than last year; our manager is always stressed. It's times like this when you want to throw in the towel—and when you ask for help, the most common advice you receive from others is, "Be positive" and, "Look on the bright side." Often, this type of generic advice that neglects practical counsel can escalate the stress or pain that you are feeling even more.

Tough times may not be as tough as we think and it is important that we put things into perspective. I can remember when I started my first door-to-door business and had secured a contract with a pay-TV client. Despite the difficulty of the task ahead, my lack of experience and young age supplied me with all of the enthusiasm in the world and a welcomed overdose of confidence.

I needed to assemble a team of professional direct salespeople. I had it all worked out; I had put out job advertisements, conducted interviews and got people inspired to join my team. I went and booked a professional training facility, developed my own content, printed workbooks, designed flashy PowerPoint slides—and I was ready to start my business. In my opinion, day one of the induction was a roaring success. Unfortunately, that opinion wasn't shared by anyone else. From the six people whom I originally hired, two of them had left by afternoon tea, one didn't turn up the next day, and by lunchtime on the second day they were all gone. I could not have imagined a greater crisis than this. It was horrible. I was not going to achieve my sales targets for another month, I would have to face the company, whose products I was selling, and explain my failure. I would spend the next few weeks alone at night knocking doors.

I remembered getting in the car and going to see my business at-the-time mentor, Tristan Robinson. Tristan and I sat down over a coffee and I offloaded all my angst, pain, loss and frustration. To me this was like the end of the world and I was ready to quit.

Cleverly enough, Tristan did not speak. He let me empty my cup without the slightest nod or affirmation to validate my emotions. After I had finished speaking, he looked me right in the eye and said, "Sana, it's just a job. This is just an experience." He let a moment pass and allowed time for me to think about it. He followed on by asking, "In 18 months' time, will you still be stressed about this moment?" To which I responded, "Of course not." "Well, if it is not going to be important in 18 months", Tristan continued, "chances are that it's not that important now. Put it into the perspective of the overall picture. This is a fleeting moment in a series of countless ups and downs that define our lives. Focus on what you can control—and move on."

Tristan asked me to list everything from this situation that I was concerned about, which I did. Then we prioritised a list based on the activities that I was able to influence and disregarded the rest. Once I completed this exercise, my thoughts were collected and my plan of action was clear. A lot of the elements that initially seemed uncontrollable were in fact in my control. I could control the quality of my training, I could constructively take on the feedback, I could ensure that I maintained a resourceful attitude, and I could make enough sales to supplement my loss of income in the next few weeks.

Since that moment, which was many years ago, I have never again felt the urge to vent. I am quickly able to identify a crisis, apply this model to myself and turn it into a victory.

Momentary ups and downs in sales (and life) are natural, so we should not dwell unnecessarily on these times and give up over a bad week. Putting your situation in perspective and stepping outside of your emotive state are powerful techniques in preventing the impact of a downturn in sales.

Now reflect on a time when you experienced a work crisis or a drop in sales results. Step outside of your situation and view yourself from an objective third-person perspective. How did you respond? What advice would you give yourself? What will you do differently if this happens again? What questions will you ask yourself to catapult you out of the slum and into a resourceful state of mind?

OUR IDENTITY IS EVERYTHING

Have you ever heard the saying, "If you believe in yourself, you can achieve anything"? Some may feel that such a phrase is just a false sense of motivation and that we should be more realistic about our approach to success; however, having an effective and useful mindset is not just an theoretical concept. It is in fact critical to one's success. Without taking this saying into extremes, we should see the truth in it. Think of this in simple terms: if I believe that *I am not a salesperson*, then guess what? I won't sell. If I don't believe that I am management material, then I will never apply for a management position, and therefore never be a manager. These beliefs shape our identity and determine the type of success we will have.

Unfortunately, this somewhat intuitive thinking is not how sales performance is managed. Very rarely does one focus on someone's identity to boost sales as it seems far too distant from the sale. Instead, we tend to spend more time focusing on the outcomes alone. I can distinctly remember when my managers were trying to stretch my performance by saying, "Get me some more sales," "Top the leader board," or, "Make sure you are better than Peter!" What kind of advice was that? Don't they think that if I knew how to be better, then I would?

Frank Romano, the developer of *Precision Selling*, explores this concept through the Success Spiral. The Success Spiral teaches us how to change our results by focusing on the drivers towards those outcomes, rather than on the outcomes themselves.

The first noteworthy insight to the Success Spiral is that you are not your results ('identity' $\neq$ 'results'). When you are passionate about what you do, it is very easy to feel that your value as an individual is based on your output. Our managers, friends and peers often feed this perception by labelling us on our results—"You are a gun," or, "You are terrible." One may argue that these statements are true; however, just because you have positive sales results does not mean that you are categorically an amazing person. Similarly, if you are poor at selling, it does not indicate you are less of a person. We are not our results and we must not fall into the trap of believing this, as it will heavily impact our chance of success. We need to separate identity and results by seeing how they drive each other, rather than equal each other.

The Success Spiral shows how our *identity* influences our *actions*; that is, our efficacy towards an activity will be determined by our belief in ourselves. If we see ourselves as a champion salesperson, we will confidently approach the most challenging sales conversations. If we believe that we are a novice salesperson, we will refrain from handling objections and going for big deals. Those actions then lead to proportionate results; that is, if you perform like a champion, you will move closer to champion results, and if you perform the way a novice would, then the equivalent results will follow.

Once we achieve a *result*, be it favourable or not, we give ourselves a self-assessment in the form of a *story* that justifies the result. We could tell ourselves, "Wow, I am very good at this," or, alternatively, "I was really bad," based on our perception of the outcome. These stories that we tell ourselves directly influence our identity, which then leads to an action, a result and another story—and hence a self-perpetuating spiral begins.

At all times we are either spiralling up by reaffirming our identity through positive stories or spiralling down using stories built on negative foundations.

To illustrate the Success Spiral with an example, I want to challenge every reader of this book to a game of snooker. No, seriously! I want to challenge any of you to a game of snooker, and I can already guarantee the outcome... You will win! I am potentially one of the worst snooker players in the world. Being the worst snooker player began well before I even picked up my first cue. Picture this: I was having dinner with a group of friends from my university years. As we were catching up on old times and having a few laughs, the owner of the house mentioned that he had a snooker table and suggested a two-on-two match. While everyone was excited, I, on the other hand, felt a cold sweat starting to run from the top of my forehead. Stories were racing through my mind: "Am I any good at this?" and, "I hope I don't suck," and, "These guys play all the time," and, "I am not a snooker player!"

We finished dinner, left the plates behind and everyone rushed to the snooker table. As I walked cautiously behind them, I approached the table and Adam threw me the cue and asked me to take the first hit. I made a series of excuses that were all shot down and it was my turn to play and face my fears.

How do you think my identity was shaping up before I had even taken my first shot? Would I have labelled myself as a beginner? An enthusiastic learner, perhaps? No—all I thought was, "I have no idea what I am doing—I hope my friends don't laugh too much"(stories), and, "I am really bad at this" (identity). Do you think that this identity influenced a certain behaviour or action and result? Of course it did. I barely took it seriously nor did I try my best (action). Snooker balls were flying off the table, balls were being missed altogether and my team mate was getting frustrated (result). As I put the cue down and walked away from the table, my internal dialogue began getting louder and louder. I started telling myself negative stories about how much of a horrible and embarrassing snooker player I was (stories). My identity? The world's worst snooker player. Imagine how I took my next shot— and the spiral continued.

These stories reaffirmed pre-existing beliefs that I had about myself. My identity was no longer a perception; I believed it to be reality. I was on a downward spiral, rapidly heading towards continuous failure! So how does one get out of this downward spiral?

The answer: by adjusting the most controllable part of the Success Spiral—your stories. When you get an undesirable outcome, it is difficult to change the outcome without increasing the effectiveness of your actions—and your actions will not sustainably shift unless you believe that you deserve better results. Your stories, on the other hand, are an easier choice. If your outcome scores one out of ten in terms of your standards of success, then you have a choice on what story gets told, "I am learning and since other people have succeeded in this, I know that it is possible for me to," or, "Imagine how great I will be at this if I continue to practice." The impact that these stories will have on your identity will have a positive influence on your effort towards your actions, which will produce better results and now the spiral goes up.

So let's bring this back to sales. If you believe that you are not a salesperson, you can add all the skills and techniques of the world onto your tool belt and nothing will change as you will never act inconsistently to your identity. Everything pivots around our identity and our identity is influenced by our stories! Reflect for a moment on an area of development for yourself. How does the quiet voice inside describe your abilities in this area? Is it feeding the downward spiral? What stories could you tell yourself to reverse the pattern?

Remember; it's important for the stories to be real, or else you won't believe them. Don't say, "I am the world's greatest," because the unconscious mind will respond with many reasons as to why you are not. Change your stories to, "Every time I practise this, I will get better and better," "Others have succeeded, therefore I will succeed," "All the resources I need to succeed are within me," and,

"I am in a process of learning".

THE NEW SALES IDENTITY

We need to reshape the identity of salespeople, since the current perception is not consistent with the behaviours of the new breed. Salespeople should no longer need to justify their work or make excuses when someone asks about their occupation at a family barbeque. Below are some great responses that I have heard from salespeople to the question, "So, what do you do for a living?"

- I help people achieve their goals

- I add value to strangers whom I meet

- I dedicate my time to saving people money

- I help clients solve unknown problems

- I am responsible for providing tangible benefits to people who interact with my company

- I am a consultant

- I am an expert

- I help people make difficult decisions

SELF-FULFILLING PROPHECIES

After exploring the power of stories, it has become clear that our actions are consistent with our beliefs. If you believe something to be true, you will create a reality that aligns with these beliefs.

Many years ago, a group of American scientists conducted an experiment to see how beliefs impacted results. Researchers were given a set of rats and were told that one group of rats were considered smart and the others were stupid. The researchers were then asked to assess the abilities of the two groups of rats to navigate through mazes. Now, the truth is that there was no difference between the groups of rats and the experiment was not to test how well the rats learned the mazes. It was to see if the information regarding the rats' intelligence influenced the actions of the researchers.

How do you think their beliefs impacted their assessment? In actual fact, both groups of rats behaved similarly and there was no objective distinction between the groups; however, when the biased researchers saw the *smart rats* going the wrong way, they perceived them as exploring. When a *not-so-smart* rats went the wrong way, it was viewed as dumb. The misguided lens of the researchers' beliefs tainted any action performed by these rats and creative reasons were developed to validate their initial beliefs.

Salespeople are like these researchers, and we can very easily let our prejudices and beliefs about customers influence our actions; for example, if a customer approached you and your first thoughts were, "They are just browsing," or, "Great—another window shopper," or, "Such a time-waster," how do you think you would treat them? Wouldn't it be a lot more difficult to treat them with a greater degree of enthusiasm or go that extra mile to run around and source information for them? The moment you witness a glimmering of disinterest or lack of decisiveness, you accept that as reality and give up on the customer. Just like the researchers did with the so-called dumb rats. Instead, maybe the customer was indecisive because they needed time to think or showed disinterest because of something else was on their mind.

Many salespeople carry unconscious prejudices towards young people's ability to afford products, old people's ability to understand technology or certain nationalities and their likelihood to buy.

What if, however, we were able to change the stories about our customers? What if that same customer walked in and you thought, "Fantastic—every customer can benefit from the features of our products, and if this customer has made the effort to walk into our store, that means they are interested," or, "I have a responsibility to make sure that this customer can make an informed decision about our products and services," or, "My job is to bring someone closer to the buying decision than they were before they walked into the store," would this change the way you acted? How would you have responded when the customer showed slight disinterest? With resourceful beliefs, you can never give up. Instead, you may think, "What can I say now to re-engage the customer, as I have not demonstrated enough value?" and then try harder.

Our self-fulfilling prophecies are not merely limited to types of customers. When I ran a small door-to-door business many years ago, I was able forecast, almost to the exact number of sales that we would achieve, based on the wild and whacky beliefs that my team had. One team member passionately believed that only 1 in every 24 would be a sale—not as an average, but as a fact. There were countless occasions when he would have knocked at 23 doors and received 23 rejections and got the sale on the next door. On the counter, if he got a sale on the first door, then he almost always got 23 rejections to follow that. His fabricated beliefs were writing his paycheque. Another salesperson used to say, "If they have a Volvo in their driveway, they will never buy from a door-to-door salesperson." So what does he do? He avoids all houses that have a Volvo in the driveway—he had so much conviction in his beliefs that he forced them to become a reality.

As the sales manager, I quickly realised this and started focusing on people's beliefs. In the case of the salesperson who believed that only 1 in 24 houses gets a sale, I gave him the smallest street of only 8 homes (to avoid him burning 23 customers at a time) and told him about this street's receptivity to our products. I gave him statistical facts, social proof and a great deal of conviction, which resulted in him spending the whole night in this street and walking away with 4 sales—more than he had ever done before in a day.

I became so confident in this approach that I started creating stories that were so broad I felt like I was reading out their horoscope. I used to say, "If the house has a nice garden, that means they take pride in their home and your solution will add to their masterpiece"—and sales would rise. I had a useful story about every type of customer. For a period of time, I stopped training, coaching and observations. I didn't need any of those things; my team were capable of selling, as it was only their self-fulfilling prophecies and limiting beliefs that had previously stood between success and failure. Of course, these stories cannot be fictional; they need to have a logical basis or they will fail to influence beliefs.

When you start to bring your prejudices to your consciousness, you can remove these self-limiting beliefs one by one. Do not hold your success in sales at ransom to non-resourceful beliefs. Take some time to reflect on beliefs that you have about your customers, the time of year, product types and yourself that are holding you back from more success.

BELIEF TEST

How strongly do you believe in what you do, what you sell and what you represent? To help you measure your level of belief, finish the sentences and elaborate further. If you are a sales manager, you may also wish to do this with your team.

- I am passionate about the company I work for because…

- I believe in my products/services because…

- I love the work that I do because…

If this exercise was difficult, it tells us one of two things: we require more practice on this activity and in expressing our thoughts; or we simply do not believe in what we do, sell and who we represent.

BELIEVE IN YOUR PRODUCT

Genuinely believing in your product is a critical part of sales success and in making you a more authentic person. Believing in your product does not necessarily mean that you need to buy all of your company's products yourself, as it may not be feasible in many circumstances; for example, you may be selling luxury boats, and believing in your product does not need to manifest itself through ownership of a boat that you cannot afford. Believing in your product is about having a strong understanding of how these products and services positively impact our customers, and having confidence in the unique wow factors that make your product stand out from those of the competitors.

Many instances of disbelief in one's product offering come from the company's high price point. These non-useful thoughts need to be removed. Take Mercedes Benz, for example: they have been a leading organisation since 1926 without being the cheapest product on the market. How would you rate the belief of their sales staff on Mercedes Benz's products? The staff are well aware that being the price leader does mean that you have the best products, and price consciousness is a bigger deal to salespeople than to our customers.

Let's use Apple as an example of great conviction. They have megastores in major cities around the world, run by highly passionate staff. These salespeople are so passionate that, in 2012, RetailSails reported Apple making an average of $5600 per square foot of floor space in its stores annually, which is higher than any retailer in the US. The most remarkable fact about the passion of Apple Store employees is that they do not get paid a single cent of commission for their sales. In fact, financial incentives through sales commission are against Apple's business ethos. Instead, people sell their products out of sheer belief that they are the best products in the market. In *The Steve Jobs Way*, ex-Apple executive Jay Elliot tells us that the company's late co-founder Steve Jobs believed that his products would change the world and would only hire individuals who shared this belief. It was a known fact that if Jobs heard of an individual who lacked belief in Apple's products, he would personally meet them and try to understand why.

Apple's prices are high-end and some would argue that their mobile phone, the iPhone, is not as fully featured and customisable as its other smartphone competitors. The staff within the Apple Store have such belief in the superiority of their products that if you talk about their high prices, the salesperson will respond with, "It's not a cost; it's an investment." If you try to haggle with them and say, "Give me a discount or I will just wait for the next model of the iPhone to come out," they will respond with, "Okay—then wait." Trust me; I tried.

Belief helps us move some behaviours from uncomfortable to comfortable. For instance, being persistent in sales can feel confrontational and pushy; however, if you were selling a lifesaving medical procedure, you would not take no for an answer just to avoid appearing pushy. People who believe in their products show their persistence in sales through conviction and certainty, not a selfish desire win a deal. As Cavett Robert rightfully says, "The prospect is persuaded more by the depth of your conviction than he is by the height of your logic." If you can do both, you have unlocked the secrets of sales. To stay ahead of the game, we need to believe in our product more than our most loyal customers do.

BEING RIGHT ISN'T GOOD ENOUGH

While knowledge and facts are important, they are not enough to change behaviours. Alone, they can spark interest and curiosity; however, long-term mindsets and firmly established beliefs are hard to shift.

Aristotle, a renowned brilliant mind, has contributed many insights to the generations that followed him. Aristotle was not known to perform experiments to prove his philosophies; rather, he was satisfied by his observations and logical thoughts to explain the mysteries of the world and the rules of motion. The generations that followed him believed his philosophies to be true and these beliefs were hardwired into people's minds. For instance, Aristotle believed that the speed of gravity's pull was determined by the weight of an object; that is, a ten-pound ball will fall ten times faster than a one-pound ball. This was a well-known 'fact' and for many years to follow and was taught in universities.

Over eighteen hundred years later, the now famous physicist Galileo Galilei challenged this well-known *fact*. Galileo was convinced that the weight of the object did not impact the speed that it would drop. Academics at the time felt that his claim was ridiculous and aimed to ridicule Galileo. In order to quiet the support of his followers, they challenged him to prove his theory. Galileo accepted the challenge and went to the top of the Leaning Tower of Pisa with two different weights of the same material. He then dropped the two objects off the top of the tower. To the great surprise of onlookers, they landed at precisely the same time. Students and professors who witnessed the experiment were proven wrong without the least shadow of a doubt.

Following this demonstration, guess which theory the University of Pisa was teaching? That's right; they kept Aristotle's philosophy, even though it was proven wrong. This theory was completely hardwired into their belief system and they could not accept another possible position on the theories of gravity. Providing knowledge, evidence and one compelling demonstration is sometimes not enough to influence behaviour.

For this reason, we need to follow the 'know, believe, express' model.

KNOW, BELIEVE, EXPRESS

Knowing that our success hinges on our beliefs, the next milestone for a salesperson is to become a great myth-buster. Many beliefs that we hang onto about our product, organisation, industry and customers may not necessarily be true. Many of them could be myths that we have adopted from opinions in the media and objections that our customers give us. Common examples of sales myths are universal comments like, "None of our customers can afford it", "We have completely saturated the market", "Selling is manipulative" and "No one is interested." These broad statements that we feed into our belief system are detrimental to sales success and are often not backed by evidence.

Sales managers will often try to bust myths with salespeople by sharing their personal views and anecdotes in a hope to influence. Unfortunately, it takes much more than a compelling presentation of opinions to shift a mindset. The best-case outcome of using this method is hearing lip service from the salesperson or agreeing to disagree.

The 'know, believe, express' model for creating a mind shift does not come down to compelling arguments and firm opinions. To create a mind shift for someone or for ourselves, one needs to acknowledge facts (know), see evidence and proof points (believe) enough times until we are confident to share it with others (express). Galileo's story shares how much time and effort is required to cause a mindset change. Below is a breakdown of the 'know, believe, express' model that you can use on others or yourself:

- KNOW—your argument must be based on facts, not opinions. Use statistics, testimonials and independent unbiased sources

- BELIEVE—prove it, demonstrate where possible, give examples and use metaphors where needed

- EXPRESS—explain it to others, get feedback, use the facts in your explanation to validate your words, articulate your newfound learning with customers until those myths are busted with them as well

When a colleague or you have a counterproductive belief, go and do some research and explore the facts. Sales managers, if you are telling your staff that your products are the best, bring along research of what the competitors are offering and let the staff member explain to you why our products are superior. If a staff member says, "Selling is evil," "I don't like asking intrusive questions," "Customers don't like it when I sell," Are you going to tell them your customer experiences and why you love to sell? I hope not. Use the facts that we have discussed in previous sections of this chapter and don't tell them about it; read it with them—heck, I don't care if you photocopy the page. Get them to independently read the detailed information and explain it back to you. Once you have heard them express the information with conviction, you know the process of mind shift has started.

The next few sections will help us master the sales mindset.

SEE SUCCESS

If we take on a new way of thinking or approach to selling and do not see immediate results, it is unlikely that we will try it again. Remember, our previous beliefs and habits are strongly ingrained in our minds. We will grab any opportunity or slight glimmering of doubt to return to them. To sustain new beliefs, it is important that we are able to prove the facts to ourselves and see a change by adopting these beliefs.

I remember coaching a salesperson and each time that we conducted a role-play, her response was, "But I can't be as charismatic or funny as you." I knew that it was going to be an uphill battle trying to convince her that charisma and humour are not required in order to be successful in sales. I used the 'know, believe, express' model and I could see her perception start to change. After that, I wrote down two questions on a piece of paper that would alter the direction of her conversations with customers. I gave her the piece of paper and said, "If you are not confident in asking these questions, just pick up the piece of paper and read them out." Of course, I do not normally recommend reading to a customer; however, she needed to see success without showmanship, so drastic measures were needed.

With slight frustration and a strong desire to prove me wrong, she grabbed the piece of paper, held it up in front of the next customer and with a bland voice started reading. To her great surprise, the customer responded with energy and openness, which carried the conversation forward and resulted in a sale. She saw success with her own eyes, believed that charisma and humour is not a requirement for sales success—and never forgot it. Seeing success soon after a mind shift is critical to locking in the new beliefs.

When you try something new or adopt new beliefs or behaviours, it will feel uncomfortable and the initial execution will be clunky. Don't try it once and assess it there. Try out the new mindset, theory or sales practice until you see success. If it is not working after multiple attempts, get feedback from others, because it may be that your myths and stories are creeping back in and impacting your actions.

THE WORLD NEEDS SALESPEOPLE

Alec Robinson is not a salesperson; he is an inventor. That's right—Alec from Australia has an occupation with two aspects: see a need and then fulfil a need. In his career, Alec has invented many amazing products that fulfil people's needs. His inventions include protective caps to prevent ladies' nail varnish from chipping, a skateboard that exerts low impact on rider's knees, a four-pronged hairdryer and even the world's first electric cradle. So why have you never heard of these inventions or heard of Alec Robinson? That's right: Alec is not a salesperson. So why does the world need him to be?

In the last decade, Australia has suffered some severe bushfires. In 2003, approximately 3.5 million hectares of land was burnt down consisting of over 540 homes, and in 2006 a further 100 homes were destroyed. At various times, each state in Australia implemented laws stating that all homes and buildings must be fitted with smoke alarms to ensure that these fires could be detected early, to save people's lives. Did it work? In many cases, yes, as smoke alarms woke families in the middle of the night for them to make a timely escape away from the blaze. In 2007, however, Victoria experienced the most deadly bushfire in its recorded history. The 36-day fire that was later named Black Saturday was responsible for burning down over 4000 homes and structures and ended the lives of 173 people. So why did these alarms not work if they detect early signs of fire?

Smoke alarms installed inside houses can detect smoke within the house—which is not useful in the case of a bushfire. A bushfire starts from outside the home, and in many cases starts from the roof and makes its way down. By the time the fire has penetrated the tiled or tin roof and the structure of the ceiling to produce smoke near the inner ceiling of a home, it is, unfortunately, too late. It was tragedies like this that inspired Alec Robinson to put pen to paper and invent a solution. At a minimal cost to himself and the end customer, the smoke detectors Alec developed were to be fixed to the inner side of the roof tiles. When the device detects smoke creeping in from the outside of the house, it sets off, waking the household and saving their lives. Great invention, right?

Well, unfortunately, in the case of a bushfire, you will not have one of these detectors installed in your roof, because Alec Robinson struggled to sell the concept. For over seven years, he has been pitching to some of Australia's largest security companies who own a significant share in the smoke alarm industry—but they didn't buy.

Even though this is a great invention and one that few people would argue against, there is not a flash mob of people who are going to run up to Alec's door and just buy it. Concepts need to be explained and people need to be engaged. Thomas Edison did not just invent the electric light-bulb and people dived at the idea— Edison struggled to get people to even view the product. So he installed electricity in an office building for free just to grab people's attention. Edison learnt to become a salesperson.

Remember, the world needs salespeople to help us see value in the things that benefit us. Be proud of your profession and skill—it is needed.

4 CONNECTING WITH THE CUSTOMER

RAPPORT—WHAT IS IT GOOD FOR?

Have you ever walked into a store knowing what you wanted and then not buying it because the salesperson was rude or somewhat unnerving? On the other hand, have you ever walked into a store as a window shopper and ended up buying something from a great salesperson because you had a connection with them? Most of us have experienced both. Adopting the perspective of a customer perspective reminds us how important rapport is to the sales process. As a salesperson, you may have the most detailed product knowledge and the most tuned mindset, accompanied by a well-constructed formula of questions and the power to articulate benefits; however, if your customer doesn't like you, trust you, believe you or care about your message, you will go nowhere. In fact that customer would rather walk away from you and endure the inconvenience of waiting for the next opportunity to buy that product or service. As mentioned before, our customers are alert and conscious of what to expect from salespeople and will not settle for anything less. As Josh Kaufman reminds us in *The Personal MBA*: think of customers as the boss who can fire you at any time. If you understand this, you will know how to treat your customers.

IMPORTANCE OF BEING LIKED

A few years ago, I went into a car dealership half serious about buying a brand-new car. As I walked into the showroom, a salesperson approached me and without any hesitation, went straight for the kill with his clearly scripted sales pitch. He looked e up-and-down, started making bold assumptions about me and, without asking questions, recommended a sports car that he described as an "awesome ride". I told him that I wasn't interested in a sports car, considering that I drive in traffic in the mornings and would find no use for a fast car. So what did he do? Did he change his approach? Did he stop and try and learn more about me? No. With even greater enthusiasm, he stuck by his guns and continued recommending the sports car. He used every objection handling and closing tactic under the sun, from surprise and delight; demonstrating all of the unknown features of the sports car to making me feel cheap for not buying. I went from half serious to completely disinterested.

As I was walking out of the dealership, another salesperson chased me to the door in an attempt to open the door for me. As I approached the door, he asked "Sir, before you leave, let me ask you a question: when buying a car, what's important to you?" He got my attention. This question intrigued me to begin a conversation. I told him I wanted a car with leather seats, sunroof, parking sensors and heated seats. To be honest, I was on a roll; I was chatting away and told him everything. He wrote it all down, listened to my requests, laughed at my jokes and—guess what? I liked him. As a customer, I went from half serious to hearing him out and ended up buying a new car on the spot.

Being liked is incredibly important. In many cases, it is the difference between success and failure in the game of sales. So how do we get people to like us without being cheesy and over the top? The answer to the question all comes down to the principles of friendship that form at a very early stage in our lives.

Imagine yourself walking through a high school during lunch where all of the students are out in their groups. The first thing that I remember, thinking back, is that the students were distinctly defined into segments. We have nerds, gothics, smokers, skaters and, remarkably, even good-looking girls find a way to form a single group. These groups are naturally formed and you very rarely see one 'human type' mixed with the others; that is, a nerd and a football hero were not walking to class together. So how did this happen? Who created the rule that said that all people wore black clothing and dark make-up needed to be in the same group? Think about your own group of friends. I am sure that there is something strong that binds you. Are you in the same neighbourhood? Speak a common second language? Participate in the same hobby? Perhaps, look similar to each other?

The principle behind this phenomenon is simple and not one that this author invented: people like people who are like themselves. Are we that obsessed with ourselves that we only spend time with people who are like us? Sadly, yes. Whether we like to admit it or not, it is proven that we are our own biggest fans. We love ourselves that much that we seek people that resemble us. We consider them as 'normal' people.

This principle is not exclusive to us; our customers are the same—they like people like themselves. In order to be liked, therefore, we need to be more like them. So how can I be like them and still be me? Is there a balance?

BE YOURSELF

Do you remember going for your first job interview? You would have been quite nervous, or perhaps naively confident. You planned out your outfit, your introduction, the strength of your handshake and the answers to some curly questions. In many cases, you will have sought out advice from a friend, family member or someone with interview experience and asked, "How should I act in the interview?" or, "What kind of person do you think they're looking for?" The vast majority of the time, the advice sounds like this: "Don't worry—just be yourself."

Good advice, right? Wrong! Unfortunately, the advice of 'just be yourself' is some of the worst advice someone can ever give you, because it is often misunderstood. Does this contradict the tag line of this book, which is to 'succeed in sales by being you'? No.

Being yourself can mean different things to different people, based on their levels of awareness. Think about it now: what does *being you* look like? For many of us, our minds will be drawn back to our most comfortable self, when we are relaxing with your friends and family. Is this really the person you want to display in front of a future employer or your customers?

It is very important when we self-reflect that we have enough objectivity and detachment to step outside of our own bodies and observe ourselves. If you do this, you will very quickly see that there are already many versions of 'you' already. There is the you who goes to work, visited grandparents, gives a speech, talks on the phone, talks to themselves, gets angry, acts silly. These versions of 'you' are not something that we need to force; we naturally introduce these versions of ourselves to the world without any coaching or someone else prompting us.

Think about how you act in front of the elderly. You are more gentle, respectful, sensitive and mature. Your sense of humour changes, your commentary of the world is filtered and your expectations of those individuals are different. Now picture yourself with a baby. How do you speak? Do you walk differently? Do you crawl with them and make funny noises? Why do we do this? Are we fake and insincere individuals? No—we are merely adapting to the situation. One thing that remains the same in all of those scenarios is that you were still *you*, just with different behaviours.

For some reason, however, salespeople often fall into two different characters when they interact with customers. They either act too formally and throw the customer off, or take their friends' advice literally and act too relaxed, hoping everyone likes their comfortable personality. Remember, you can change your behaviour and still be you.

Salespeople have employed many methods in order to get customers to like them. One school of thought is that you need to mirror the customer's personality and share their interests to show the customer that you are like them. You will mirror their tone, body language and preferences. If executed correctly, it can be a very powerful tool. On the other hand, you may not necessarily like their preferences and you can come across as insincere. Remember our customers are not oblivious to this, and any glimpse of dishonesty will put you in the same category as all typical salespeople, with the result that rapport is lost. The other danger with this practice is that you may mirror negative behaviours. If the customer approaches and you says, "I hate your company and everything it stands for," should your response be, "Yeah, me too... we stink."? Of course not.

Another school of thought that you can read more about in

Malcolm Gladwell's *Tipping Point* is that when two people enter into a conversation, they engage in a dance. When you dance with a partner, you do not merely mimic their actions in order to stay in sync. Instead, you move and flow as you hear the music, in what may appear as structured chaos. Dynamic conversations are where people are in flow; tone, body language, pitch and volume fall into conversational harmony. As Gladwell describes, this is what we often refer to as 'clicking' with someone.

Whichever rapport technique you subscribe to, there are common principles that we should always observe in order to establish and maintain rapport. Firstly, we should match the customer's level of intensity or engagement when they are speaking about a topic; for example, if the customer walks in and passionately says, "I hate your company and everything it stands for," with an equal surge of passion you could say, "Customer satisfaction is our biggest priority, so I am very eager to find out why you feel this way and how we can improve our service to you." On the other hand, if the customer is introverted and shows little to no enthusiasm, you do not want to be over the top with excitement and passion for your brand. Instead, we can use the power of facts and logical reasoning to create interest.

The second core principle that should be followed is to always show interest—though not necessarily to agree. If someone tells you that they love golf and you despise the sport, you can still show interest in their passion without having to fake liking the sport. Use your higher feelings of interest in the customer to ask open-ended questions and delve further. If you are not interested in what customers have to say and don't value their conversations, then you're in the wrong business!

MORE THAN JUST CHIT-CHAT

One will often hear salespeople define rapport as the discussion of common interests such as the weather, the weekend, a local sporting team, hobbies and interests. This brief chit-chat can certainly contribute to elements of the rapport-building process; however, it is not the process itself. Rapport is not merely founded on one's ability to make continuous and interesting small talk—it is much more than that. Rapport requires a genuine connection founded on trust and a mutual understanding between individuals.

Chit-chat and talking favourite sports cars will, unfortunately, not be enough to turn a stranger into a friend.

For most people in sales, the rapport-building process does not require you to know the intricacies of every customer's family history in order to connect. The degree of the rapport that is required in a salesperson/customer relationship will depend on the type of commitment you are asking from the customer—the greater the investment from the customer, the greater the rapport.

In fast paced-environments like call centres or shopping centres, customers do not have either the time or the patience for long conversations—so we need to get straight to the point. In order to do this, we should focus our conversations on topics that are relevant to the solution we can provide. If you are an accountant, building rapport is less about talking sports, and more about talking upcoming financial commitments like holidays, buying a car or sending children to a private school. Likewise, if you were selling a car repair service, a great conversation would be around all of the cars that they have owned.

Customers are weary of mindless chatter that goes nowhere, such as, "So, how's ya day?" or, "I love your bag, it's really nice." They believe you don't care, even if you do. Keeping the conversation relevant will avoid the customer thinking, "Why on earth are you asking me that?"

JOINING THEIR MODEL OF THE WORLD

One of the greatest barriers to building genuine rapport is being stuck in your own model of the world. Staying in your model of the world is where we observe reality through our own limited lens and not through the eyes of others. Being stuck in this position is not something that exclusively takes place in our minds. It manifests in our language, our questions and our behaviours. It does not take a trained psychologist to spot this either. Our customers can see these qualities, and as soon as they recognise that their needs are not the primary focus of the conversation, they will switch off.

You may have seen these salespeople before or even caught yourself making this mistake. When we fall into this trap, we become blinded and always talk about the features of the product that we like; we are thinking about our commission during the conversation, and our primary goal is to close the sale. My wife and

I recently went to a travel agent to book a holiday to New York. From our perspective, we were only there to get a quote and compare it with the prices online. The salesperson, on the other hand, was stuck in her world and was solely focused on closing the deal. After 45 minutes of the conversation, we asked her to print out a quote for us to review. With a look of disgust, the travel agent said, "Excuse me—you guys have been unfair. I have spent almost an hour looking up flights for you. The least you can do is give me a $150 deposit for the flight." This poor girl was so trapped in her own model of the world, that she failed to see the situation from our perspective and lost the sale. We went out of our way to give the same flight to another agent.

To be a master of effective sales conversations, we need to start with the customer's perspective in mind. We should find an appreciation for each customer's buying behaviour. Some like to make quick decisions; some need to ask family; some will conduct extensive research. For instance, salespeople like to quickly end awkward silences with a comment or another benefit. Before we do this, we should ask ourselves, who are these silences awkward for? Do the customers tell us that silence makes them uncomfortable? Generally, silences are only awkward for the salesperson. If we join the customer's model of the world, we realise that silences may be necessary for the customer to digest all of the information and make a decision. The more we interrupt this, the more times we will get the following outcome: "I need to think about it." Of course they need to *think about it*—they were trying to do just that when a salesperson interrupted their silence!

When we are conscious of the customer's perspective, we are able to adjust our language and the structure of our conversation to accommodate the stage that the customer is in. Failing this, we would be closing too early, asking inappropriate questions, making poor assumptions or not finding the balance between being direct and indirect.

When we join the customer's model of the world, we are able to focus on solving their problem, which will lead to a satisfied buyer.

THE NEW GOLDEN RULE

Many of are familiar with the Golden Rule: treat people the way that you would want to be treated. This is a well-intentioned rule, and one that many salespeople abide by; however, does this not indicate that we are approaching things from our own model of the world? What if we were very time-poor and always wanted to be spoken to with urgency—does this mean that we should impose this upon everyone we meet? On the other hand, if I like to be greeted with a high five, should I do the same for my grandmother?

We should not treat people the way we want to be treated. Instead we should treat people the way they want to be treated. This new paradigm has been coined as the Platinum Rule.

When we speak to our customers, we should invest the time to learn about how they think, speak, decide and buy. Once we know this, we can align our conversation style and behaviour to their preferences and connect with them. Certain customers would prefer to be referred to as 'sir', while others as 'mate' or 'buddy'—which one you decide to use can make a great difference.

Of course, at the beginning of the relationship, you may not know how the customer would like to be treated. In this case, remain neutral until you have enough information to do otherwise.

OBSERVATION SKILLS

We know that rapport is about viewing the world through the same lens as another person and having mutual understanding—so how do we know what to talk about when we just meet someone for the first time? We can't just ask people, "What topics get you interested when having conversations with strangers?" Instead we should use our common sense and make sharp observations that can provide us some clues for relevant and interesting conversation starters.

In a one-on-one coaching session I had with a lady who works in real estate, we were talking about the act of prospecting. This is one of the most difficult and uncomfortable activities for real estate agents as they sometimes go door-to-door to influence people to put their house on the market. This type of conversation would require strong rapport and trust between the surprised customer and the agent. The opening words and initial conversation needs to be relevant, natural and about the customer (the most important topic to them). So how can we use our observation skills to uncover clues that would spark a great conversation with the customer? Imagine that you are walking down a residential street and you start observing a house from the street. What do you see? You see a car, a garden, style of home, mailbox, curtains, shoes, welcome mats, a basketball ring. Depending on the acuteness of your observation skills, you may actually see the condition of the car, the level of detail of garden hedges, type of curtains used, detailing of home design, number of shoes, together with their types and sizes. Observations are not limited to what you see. You may be able to capture the scent of the flowers as you walk up the driveway or smell of dinner being cooked.

So what does all of this mean to the prospecting real estate agent? Let's dig deeper on a few of them. If the customer has a really nice luxury car, we immediately know that they like to show their wealth and enjoy the finer things. If they have a people mover coupled with a big enough house, we may consider the possibility that there is a family inside the house. If the gardens are well kept, we know that they take pride in their home. If the gardens are messy, then they might not be as attached to their home. If we see shoes out the front, they might be work boots that tell us a tradesperson lives here. If the shoes are small, perhaps there are children in the home. Of course, all of these are assumptions about the customer, but they are safe ones.

If we observe well kept gardens and say, "I can see that you have dedicated a lot of time to these gardens and it's paying off— they look fantastic," we have successfully connected with the customer on a topic that is important to them.

If we have observed that there are younger children in the house and we knock on the door and start yapping on with some sales pitch, the customer might be thinking, "Gosh, I don't have time for this... Where are the kids... Are they being looked after?... The kids are sleeping; why is this salesperson being so loud?" Therefore, instead of continuing on with the conversation, we could begin by asking, "Before we continue speaking, do you need to attend to your children? I'm happy to wait." In the eyes of a parent, their children are the most important thing in their lives and if you acknowledge how special they are, you will immediately establish a mutual understanding and trust.

Remember, rapport is not about our ability to make great conversations; it is about seeing the world through the customer's perspective.

RAPPORT IS A PROCESS, NOT AN EVENT

For many years, the sales process has been described in stages and steps—for example, the seven stages of selling, the four-step sales model or the three-step sales cycle. Despite the fact that selling involves a dynamic and sometimes unpredictable conversation, there are of course distinct stages. This method of teaching sales is simple and can be effective. The unfortunate part of this type of training is not the methodology itself; rather it is how it is interpreted and practised. These various sales models can create an event-based mindset, which misleads the salesperson to assume that once a step, such as building rapport or asking questions is finished, we stop that activity entirely and move on to the next stage.

It is for this reason that many salespeople understand rapport building as that thing that we do at the beginning of the sales conversation; however, rapport is not an isolated event. Rather, it is an ongoing process that develops and builds before, during and after the sale. It is not something that we merely establish and move on from. We establish, maintain and continue to build rapport to strengthen the levels of trust and likability.

Rapport building must remain top-of-mind throughout the conversation, in the same way it does when we are talking to our close friends. Even though we think that we are completely comfortable with them, we are conscious not to cross lines and we manage our character; behaving in a manger that reflects the closeness of the relationship.

STAYING ON YOUR A-GAME

In an eight-hour shift of work, it is very easy to slip in and out of your best rapport-building state. So what's the big deal? Imagine that, during your eight-hour shift, you drop the ball for one hour and in that hour a customer walks into your store and you don't even acknowledge him/her or look up to say hello. This customer will immediately judge your abilities, which creates a lasting feeling about the brand. So what? It is just one customer, right?. Would the severity of the situation change if I told you that this customer was a journalist writing about your store or a mystery shopper, or the CEO of your company? It's easy to be on your A-game with people who matter—and if, like me, you believe that all customers matter, we should aim to always be on our A-game.

The fact is, regardless of who your customer is, you should treat him/her as if they were the CEO or someone you regard as important. Think about how you would treat the head of your company if they walked in to buy from your store. You would greet them, ask questions, be incredibly helpful; you would be enthusiastic, you would show pride in the brand and have the biggest smile on your face. Now, imagine if we were able to give every customer that same treatment. Do you think your sales might increase? Of course they would.

If this is a struggle for you to do, perhaps you can ask yourself, "Do I really care about my customers or am I just putting on an act?" Don't wait for your company to send in mystery shoppers to assess you. Being on your A-game all day isn't supposed to be easy—that's why you are in sales and not just anyone else. Recognise that every customer is as important as the next, and you will not only stay on your A-game; you will also win in the game of sales.

INTENTIONS CAN ONLY TAKE YOU SO FAR

Genuinely caring for a customer is an important element in creating rapport, and also a hard one to coach. Generally, those who are making the shift from service to sales or those who wish to succeed in sales without turning into a traditional salesperson find this easy. For those of you who fit into this category of 'caring for your customers', you may have experienced a time where you had great intentions for the customer, truly caring for their well-being, and they respond with, "You're just trying to sell me something." This can be very frustrating, as the customer has misread your intention to help.

The reason for this is simply because having good intentions alone is not enough. You could have nothing but the best of intentions; however, if they are not visible to the customer, they lose their power. It is one thing to care for our customers; it's another thing to show them that you care. The same applies to listening to the customer: it is meaningless unless we show them that we are listening.

Remember; skills and genuine intentions go hand in hand. One without the other is a recipe for a lost sale.

LISTENING

Listening sounds like a pretty straightforward skill; however, there is a defined level of consciousness that separates hearing from listening. Have you ever had a conversation with someone and just completely zoned out? Or has somebody said to you, "I know that you heard me—but were you listening?" In day-to-day conversations, people may not always notice if your mind wanders; however, in a sales conversation, customers will pick up on this very easily. They may see your eyes glance elsewhere; you may distracted by typing or writing—or, worse, you respond to their questions/comments with an irrelevant statement. If we are not listening, then we are ignoring the customer, which is guaranteed to shatter the foundations of trust and rapport. Good salespeople don't just speak better than the rest; they listen carefully and hear the clues that bad salespeople miss out on.

At school you may have been taught to practise 'active listening', where you give eye contact and nod when someone is talking. Unfortunately, this is an out-dated practice. Think about when you are talking to your closest friend or someone you really look forward to speaking to. On a micro level, what do you do in that conversation? Do you simply nod and smile to show you care? I doubt it. Instead, your eyes are wide open in fascination or you are squinting in deep concentration; your facial expressions are synced to the nature of the story; you are asking open questions in order for the speaker to elaborate, and your responses are related to the topic. If we want to show our customers that we care, we need to adopt those same natural techniques. Most salespeople are never listening; instead they are just waiting for their turn to talk. This is one of the worst habits of a salesperson.

To prevent this, we should practise by pausing for a moment right after the customer has spoken. This ensures that the customer has finished speaking and gives you a chance to digest what they have said.

Some salespeople like to summarise the customer's comment and repeat it back to them. There is value in doing this from time to time, to show the customer that you have listened and understood; however, please don't overdo this—it can become very tedious and annoying if practised too frequently.

It is true that listening builds trust; however, the skill of listening is not only performed to make our customers like us. The information the customer provides you with during general conversation, questions and objections are very useful tools in sales. You will go very far in earning the customer's respect and capturing their attention if you use their words throughout your presentation.

SAY MY NAME, SAY MY NAME

As the pop group Destiny's Child once put it, "Say my name, say my name". This successful girl group must have known about a powerful tool when building rapport—people love to hear their own name. A person's name is the sweetest sound that can hit their eardrums. As my wife sees me typing this, she quickly reminds me what the song is actually about.

I love observing people when their name has been mentioned. If a senior manager in your workplace is giving a speech at a conference and he/she acknowledges the efforts of your team, you feel good. If they point at you specifically and say "well done", you feel great. As soon as they mention your name, there is a little tingle inside. Do you know how I know this? It's the same for everyone. I go out of my way to watch people's reactions when their names get called out; regardless of their level of confidence, they can't help but readjust their seating, they swallow saliva, take a sip of water or shift their body language.

Major Australian airline QANTAS knows the magic of using names. In an online engagement campaign in 2012, they held a competition asking people to submit their photos and their names. What was the prize? An all-expenses-paid flight to the Maldives? No. Maybe a domestic flight? No. Perhaps one night in a hotel? Not even. The prize was to have their name written on the side of a plane, as a part of their 'You're the reason we fly' campaign. That's a prize? Are people really that obsessed with their names that they would enter a competition for a chance to see their name written? Yes, they are!

Using names is a great technique in building rapport. Throughout your sales conversation, during the follow-up call, and in any future communications with the customer, use their name. They will feel special when they hear it and in return they will make an effort not to forget yours.

When I attended a sales team's end-of-campaign celebration, I entered a room full of people whom I had never met. These were all members of the sales teams who had participated in the campaign my team had sponsored. Before I arrived, I invested time into memorising the names and results of the top performers and managers attending the celebration. When asked to give a few words, I mentioned the names of the people whom I was most impressed with and thanked them personally. When I left the stage, those individuals approached me to show their gratitude and told me how much they had appreciated what I did. Are you serious? You're the high achiever—I should be thanking you! And yet a simple mention of their name had compelled them to thank me. After that same presentation, a young sales manager who had not performed as well approached me and said, "Don't worry; next year you will be calling out my name on that stage." I smiled.

INTROVERT VS. EXTROVERT

There is a common perception that salespeople need to be extremely 'out there' and extroverted in order to achieve success. Well, this isn't always the case. Extremes in either extrovert or introvert behaviour are not sustainable in sales. A balanced and more measured character is far more relatable to customers and enables them to sustain a longer conversation with you.

The warning for extroverts is that customers already have perceptions about salespeople. Traditionally we are seen as ruthless, cut-throat and willing to do anything to get the sale. Your strength is an ability to excite people in loving your product; however, overplaying this strength often moves into post-purchase dissonance, where the customer regrets buying from you as they don't know why they did in the first place. As we discussed earlier, our customers are well educated in the sales process, and the slightest glimpse of this behaviour will immediately turn the customer away. Bearing in mind that some of these characteristics are a strength, we need to learn how to direct this energy into the right area. Rather than being overly excited about the product, we can be enthusiastic about meeting the needs of the customer.

Instead of speaking at one hundred miles an hour, we can listen with great passion and interest to what the customer has to say. Naturally extroverted people should learn to draw upon some introverted characteristics that are effective in selling—like being a calm, measured and an attentively listening salesperson—while directing their extroverted passion and enthusiasm towards areas that matter most to the customer. This balance will remove these fears and negative perceptions towards you.

Likewise, introverts should leverage their strengths of being patient and non-threatening, while being conscious to avoid their habits of a lack of excitement, eye contact and visible passion that make the customer doubt you and the product/service you are selling. You should therefore draw upon some extroverted characteristics like positive body language, nodding, smiling and confidence.

When aiming to connect with the customer, we should see the battle between introverts and extroverts less as innate characteristics of a person that cannot be changed and more as a behaviour that you can adjust to suit the situation. There are times where it is appropriate to be more introverted, and times to be more extroverted. These situations can depend on the product you are selling, the customer's situation, their responses, the brand you represent and the environment that you are selling in.

WHERE HAS THE TRUST GONE?

In recent times, there are people selling Russian brides, $500 PhDs and a chance to help a Nigerian Prince launder $100,000 into your bank account. It is no wonder that trust has been lost. The efforts to gain trust are immense and the potential to lose it is quite easy. Trust has become so broken that honest people are unable to be heard. In a fascinating experiment conducted by Dan Ariely and three other professors, they tested the "extent of the public's suspicion of companies". At a commercial centre in Cambridge, Massachusetts, they set up a booth with a large sign saying 'Free Money'. They had different signs indicating how much money they were giving away to each person—some reading $1, $5, $10, $20 or $50 with the corresponding denomination stacked up on the table for passers-by to see.

When they displayed the $50 sign, one would naturally imagine a large line of people queuing up to collect their free money. In actual fact, only 19% of people stopped by to ask about the free $50—while the remaining 81% saw the sign and walked on. Who wouldn't want $50 for free? It is so remarkable to see that level of scepticism exist within the majority of our consumers.

Have spam emails, irresponsible marketing and dodgy salespeople really contributed to tearing the fabric of trust in our society? Sadly, the answer is yes. So how can we stand out and become worthy of trust in a low-trust world?

WHERE DOES TRUST COME FROM?

If a customer is going to invest their own hard-earned funds into your product or service, they require a certain level of trust in not only the brand that you represent, but also in you. There are many sources of trust. One that will be discussed here is 'reliability'.

Gaining trust from the customer is more about delivering what the customer has asked for, and less about wowing them. So often I see salespeople misunderstand the concept of the saying 'under-promise, over-deliver'. People interpret this phrase as meaning, 'If a customer asks for 10 things, I will deliver 11.' More often than not, the eleventh item is not what the customer wants and these bells and whistles are not critical to the customer's decision-making process to buy, repeat business with you or to refer a friend. To gain the trust of a customer, *under promising and over delivering* means that if they have asked for 10 things, you deliver those 10 things as you promised—faster, easier and above their expectation. Reliability is hard to come by and when a customer recognises it, they will not forget it. When I was working as a consultant with a new bank in Australia, I spent a lot of time in various taxis throughout Melbourne. Taxis can be very unreliable, from the timeliness of the driver, to the type of car, to the direction in which they will drive and the price that you will pay. The very nature of taxi services can feel irregular and unsystematised compared to a train or bus. To put it simply, I don't trust taxis.

…Until I met Arshad. Arshad was a young driver who was incredibly reliable. He would turn up to my hotel or office 10 minutes earlier than I asked; he would pre-plan the direction that he would take and was able to estimate the price of the fare to within a few dollars. He treated his business seriously. He over delivered relative to my expectations. Arshad received repeat business and many referrals from me. Interestingly enough, Arshad and I spent so much time driving together that I felt impelled to reciprocate his reliability and in turn offered him business coaching. I learned that Arshad dreamed of opening his own restaurant and I invested the time in helping him get there. Only one month after my work in Melbourne, Arshad did in fact open his own restaurant in Geelong.

The trust that comes from reliability is relatively easy to gain; however, the connection is as easily broken when the reliability goes. We need to be consistent with reliability even when times are tough. Seth Godin reminds us that trust never comes from the good times and when you are simply meeting expectations. Trust is gained when it wasn't convenient; trust is gained when you told the truth when it would have been easier to lie, and you proactively kept a promise when you could have gotten away with breaking it. We should keep in mind that every challenging moment creates another opportunity to establish trust.

THE LAW OF RECIPROCITY

The inescapable and unspoken law of reciprocity demonstrates that when someone has been given something, they naturally feel impelled to give back in return. Has anybody ever gone out of their way to assist you and when they were in a time of need your natural response was to repay the favour? Have you ever assessed the size of someone's birthday present based on the size of the gift they gave you?

Reciprocity is a powerful tool. Historically, the rich created continuous power by giving to others and having people feel indebted to them. The very philosophy that drives Mafia movies is reciprocity; the Mob perform a favour in order to call upon the individual to return it one day. Professional salespeople also use the law of reciprocity to assist the sales process. Unlike the Mafia, salespeople can help their customers through reciprocity by offering them what they want. We all have unique and varying sales environments, however there are two things we can all give to the customer in order to get something in return; *our time* and *meaningful benefits*.

TIME

One of the success indicators of building rapport is the amount of time that a customer is willing to invest in you. If they are willing to give up a substantial amount of their precious time to spend with a salesperson, then you have done a good job in connecting with them.

So how do we get more time with our clients? It's simple; you must generously give time to them first. So often, salespeople are rushing customers to an outcome and not giving them the time they deserve. We must give our customers the time to share their thoughts and opinions, the time to make sound decisions, time for silences in the conversation and time to consult with other decision-makers.

When I bought my last car, the gentleman at the dealership made me a coffee as soon as we started talking. The effort to make the coffee was like a social anchor that didn't allow me to leave until we had both finished drinking. The jeweller from whom I purchased my wife's anniversary presents uses a wonderful technique in reciprocity: every time we enter his shop to browse, he immediately grabs all of my wife's jewellery and offers to clean it for her. This anchors us in his shop for at least 15 minutes to talk to him about our next big occasion.

Of course these are quick wins for the salesperson and not silver-bullet techniques. If these actions are repeated too frequently, customers will eventually become accustomed and immune to their effect.

BENEFIT

Another powerful approach to using reciprocity is giving the customer a benefit. When the customer receives a relevant benefit from you, they will naturally feel obliged to return that benefit in the form of cash to buy your product. This seems far too obvious to put in a book; however, far too often, salespeople forget to do this and waste the customer's time by rambling on about irrelevant features. This concept will be explored further in the following chapter.

GOING ABOVE AND BEYOND

As mentioned in a previous chapter, our customers are well aware of what we are trying to do. In fact they know that we receive commission, bonuses, awards and ticks on the board for every sale we make. Knowing that the salesperson will gain something from the interaction makes it challenging for customers to be genuinely grateful for how much you have helped them.

If we want to deeply connect with our customers and gain their trust, we need to help our clients in areas outside those that we earn commission from. This is where a high-integrity salesperson truly shines. Recall how you felt when a salesperson did something above-and-beyond for you, and you thought, "Wow—they did not have to do that." Would you trust this salesperson enough to repeat business or refer your friends?

Imagine a real estate agent who sells a house and then after the sale gives the client a list of the top five local schools in which to enrol their children. Or the doctor who calls you a week after an appointment to see if you are feeling better. Think about the clothing salesperson who gives advice on what outfits you can wear your new clothes with after you have bought them, or the hairdresser who spends extra time with you to explore different styles while only charging for one haircut. These customer experiences are unforgettable and become worthy of word-of-mouth marketing.

Your sales manager may refer to this time and effort as 'unproductive' or 'time-wasting'; however, as salespeople, we should feel liberated and empowered to decide where our time is best spent to help the customer. You should feel entirely free to provide 'wows' to the customer beyond what you are paid to do.

Genuine help and true generosity will yield more business than you can handle. Salespeople can be reminded of this when reflecting on the following Buddhist proverb; "if you always give, you will never be short of anything."

DEALING WITH IRATE CUSTOMERS

When facilitating seminars on the topic of rapport, I often hear comments such as, "I am great at connecting with my customers and building strong sustainable relationships except when the customer is rude," or, "How can I possibly build rapport with someone if they are already angry?" There are two areas to be mindful of when approaching these customers: the first is shaping our mindset, and the other is around what to say or do.

In order to correctly respond to irate customers, we need to adopt the correct and most useful perception of reality. The fact that you are reading this book suggests that you are not the kind of person to proactively upset customers. As such, we can safely assume that the customer's behaviour is not about you. Customers have better things to do than to hold personal grudges against an individual with whom they do not have a relationship. The customer is not trying to emotionally wound you—they are the ones who are feeling pain and are merely expressing this to you. When someone is angry or frustrated, their logical defence shields are down and their emotional weapons are at the ready.

For some strange reason, I have found that people in customer services/sales have adopted the mindset of, "Since I am the professional/expert, I need to be respected and spoken nicely to." Unfortunately, this is not the case; it is not the customer's job to be nice to us. It is our job to maintain rapport with them. In fact, we get paid to be nice to all of our customers and cannot be selectively kind only to those who reciprocate. Courtesy and kindness is something we can expect from those with whom we already have rapport, like family and colleagues. Getting this treatment from the customer should be seen as a bonus.

The final useful mindset worth adopting is to clarify the statement of 'the customer is always right'. This phrase has been used for many years, to encourage us to adopt a humble attitude of service with the customer. There is certainly some truth in this saying; however, we must explore it further in order to gain a more accurate understanding. The customer is certainly right about how they feel—nobody can correct them on this. If this customer is angry or feels cheated, we have no right to belittle or trivialise this by using facts about our products and services. Whether or not this feeling was a complete misunderstanding, it is still real, so acknowledge it. On the other hand, the customer typically will not have more knowledge on your products, services, policies and procedures than you; therefore, if the customer says that your product costs $100 and you know it only costs $50, they are not right. This is where we will also need to sensitively correct the customer's statements by clarifying.

This nuance in terms of the 'being right' concept allows us to avoid breaking company policies, giving away too much and driving the business into the ground in the name of good customer service. Stand firm and tall for what your company believes in, with a genuine care about the way the customer feels.

Lastly, when a customer is complaining or acting in an irate manner, this should be seen as an opportunity to shine. To a salesperson, irate customers are your ultimate test of skill, and when you can overcome this customer behaviour, you should feel a sense of accomplishment, much like an athlete facing their fiercest opponent. We should therefore see compliant and friendly customers as simple qualifiers, and irate customers as a championship challenge that shows off our abilities as great sales and service professionals.

So now that we have the mindset, what do we do?

To start, perhaps I can reflect on some observations of salespeople and explain what not to do. We should not try to deal with irate customers by trapping the customer in a corner through compelling arguments and focusing on proving them wrong. This method has the reverse effect, resulting in more arguments, putting the customer on the defensive and escalating emotion. All of these outcomes should be avoided at all costs.

In any hostile situation, the easiest way to defuse the tension is to provide the aggressor with the opposite response to what they are expecting. When an irate customer approaches, you need to listen attentively—not the type of listening where we are just waiting for our turn to interject, but the type of listening that is suggested earlier in this chapter. When an irate customer walks into your store or calls you on the phone, they have a mentally prepared speech that they need to express. Shutting this down, even if it is with kindness, will only further fuel the fire that is raging within them. If anything, we should do the opposite and ask for them to clarify, expand on their complaint, open-up and share more details. Ensure that they have had adequate time to express themselves or else it will remain bottled up.

How can we expect to genuinely help them if we are not willing to listen? It is only at this point that we can learn about what is concerning them and therefore find an appropriate solution. If you recognise a situation where the customer has been mistreated or that could have been better handled, then call it out: "I do apologise that this has happened to you, and to ensure that I have understood this correctly [summarise the issue]." Alternatively, in a situation in which you can see that your company has not done wrong, "I recognise that you're unhappy with regard to this situation and I am committed to making sure you walk away satisfied". This type of honesty will throw the customer off balance, as they walked into your store or called you in preparation for a fight and not expecting an empathetic listener. Once you have acknowledged some level of responsibility, where relevant, provide a solution that responds to the customer's deeper need and is fair and feasible for the organisation. Before you begin implementing the solution, ensure that it is one that the customer agrees to and don't forget to follow up.

Be honest with the customer about what you are able to do and let them know if you are going to involve others in solving the problem. This can establish realistic expectations about the amount of time and effort required to solve the problem. The customer will appreciate this level of care, which may have lacked in their last interaction. If you can strengthen relationships with these vocal customers and keep them happy, they can eventually become your greatest advocates.

SEEKING MORE BUSINESS THROUGH RAPPORT

Salespeople with integrity often have experience in customer service and are great at building rapport, developing long-lasting relationships and gaining compliments. But what are these relationships worth? Can we always quantify the value of these relationships? Some customers may return for repeat business, which is positive—however, today we can no longer run a business relying only on the same customers coming back. With the rapid rise of online shopping and the consequent fall in retail foot traffic, less and less of our customers are proactively seeking us out. Therefore, to increase the amount of customers that we interact with, we cannot simply rely on a marketing campaign or senior management to make a decision in the boardroom that will flood people through the door; we need to take responsibility for our own targets and seek our own customers.

Despite this changing reality, we know that people still like to buy from people. There are many products and services that people will not feel confident to buy online. So how do we increase our foot traffic? It's simple: once we have a rapport with the customer, we should put it into good use and ask for more business through referrals.

People who buy from you will very likely have friends who are in the same life stage, scenario and demographic as they are. Think about your last major purchase: do you have friends who may be ready to buy the same thing? Of course you do—and so do your customers. There are so many opportunities lost in sales conversations where we could proactively ask the customer if they know of anyone who would also benefit from what they are receiving. Robert Cialdini's studies in the book *Influence: The Psychology of Persuasion* reveal that the percentage of successful door-to-door sales increases impressively when the salesperson is able to mention the name of a familiar person who recommended the sales visit. We should tap into this resource and gain an ongoing flow of new business through our customers recommending their family and friends.

Rapport-building is not the only prerequisite to receiving referrals. In order to gain business from a customer's network, the following elements must be present:

CUSTOMER SATISFACTION

Requesting a customer to invite their friends to meet you should closely follow a positive moment in the sales conversation. The response will be more positive when the offer to help their friend comes following a compliment has been made about your product or service, or the customer's first satisfied use of the product. Building an association between the client's satisfaction and inviting their friends is essential as it will arm the customer with positive commentary in their conversation with their referral.

CUSTOMER ELIGIBILITY

Without asking your customer to divulge personal details about their friend, it is important to ensure that we qualify the prospective client before securing a referral. The last thing we want is to inconvenience both the customer and their friend without having an indication of the referral's eligibility to receive/use your product.

COMPELLING OFFER

There needs to be a compelling reason for the customer to give you their friend's details. Is what you have to offer better than what the referral can get on their own? Ensure that you have a compelling reason for them to tell their friends. What is it that you offer that's worth remarking about? It does not have to be a financial benefit; it could simply be your expertise, good advice or exceptional service. Empower your customer with the benefit of what their friend will gain and it will make them feel like the hero.

WARM LEAD

To avoid making the call ice-cold, ask your customer to inform their recommended friend and ensure that they know something about you before you call them.

PROSPECT'S DETAILS

For the same reason that you do not wait for Santa Claus to climb down the chimney or ask the pet store for a unicorn, you should also not expect customers who have never met you to proactively call you. So often, I see salespeople handing out business cards saying to their customers, "just ask you friend to call me and I will help her out". For this to occur, it would either be a rare case or a life-changing offer. We need to grab their friends' contact details right then and there. Don't feel that this is intrusive; let your customer be the judge of that. Remember; you are offering to help, not put them on the world's most annoying phone list that never leaves them alone.

RELEVANT SCENARIOS

The offer to help your customer's friend also to be relevant to their current situation rather than a random product-flog. We do not want to be in a situation where we are working in a pharmacy and the customer has come in to buy painkillers and we ask, "Do you have friends and family who also have headaches?" Instead, we need to wait for a scenario that offers relevance to seek more business. For instance, if a customer walks into the pharmacy asking for travel-sickness pills, you may wish to ask, "Are you travelling with others? Do you think that they might also benefit from this medication? If so, I can look after them." Any scenario that involves collective activities is a perfect set-up for such a conversation and we should be ready to capture the opportunity.

The true power behind leveraging from your customer's network of friends is that people find it very easy to resist and reject salespeople, but find it immensely more difficult to reject their friends. Good service is hard to find, so make yours exceptional and you will have advocates prospecting for you.

THE FOLLOW-UP CALL

Most salespeople feel like the battle is won once the sale is made and the customer walks out the door. If we want to remain in business for a significant amount of time, we should view sales as a continuous process and avoid looking at each sales call as a single event. This process can idealistically be defined by stages:

1. The initial sales conversation

2. Customer uses the product/service

3. Customer is satisfied

4. Customer recommends product/service to others

5. Repeat purchase

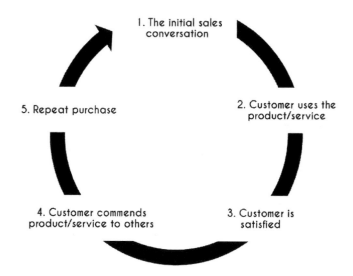

1. The initial sales conversation

2. Customer uses the product/service

3. Customer is satisfied

4. Customer commends product/service to others

5. Repeat purchase

How can we ever guarantee any achievements beyond the first stage in the absence of a follow-up call? How could we know if the customer has used the product or are satisfied? How on earth can an Internet provider, furniture salesperson, mechanic and seminar facilitator ever know if they achieved their purpose and whether or not the client will buy again? The follow-up call can lend impetus to this cycle and yield more business. When you make a follow up call, you can gauge satisfaction and alter any wrongs before the customer becomes a detractor of your product. Many objections to the product appear after the initial purchase—so imagine if they remain unhandled! When was the last time you left the doctor's office and received a follow-up call to see if you were feeling better? That would be nice, right? It seems like that should be a bare minimum in their duty of care, but it rarely happens.

Just because the follow-up call is not common, it does not make it weird or uncomfortable. If the connection is genuine, then the follow-up call is natural and expected.

YOU ARE WHAT YOU WEAR

We may wish that we lived in a world where people judged us by the quality of our work and our character; however this is not yet the reality. As shallow as it may seem, our appearance plays a big part in connecting and disconnecting from our customers. The way you choose to dress in the morning is an outward expression of how you are feeling and your competency as a salesperson.

Your clothing, grooming and overall style must be consistent with your role, the brand you represent and your customers. How could a salesperson in a bank (brand), claiming to be a financial specialist (role), for instance, greet a high-value client (customer) if they have an untucked shirt, are unshaven and have messy hair? Will customers trust, respect, like or believe this person? Unlikely. Likewise, if you are selling landscaping equipment to blue-collar tradespeople, the last thing you should be wearing is a dinner suit. A full suit-and-tie combo will disconnect you from your customers, as you do not appear as relatable.

This advice should not be confused with mirroring. For instance, if you are selling to a business, you do not necessarily need to dress as if you work there; for example, if you are selling to a plumbing service, you do not need to dress like a plumber because this creates a perception that you do not know more than they do. To sell to a business, you should dress how their advisers would dress. If you look like the people whom they are accustomed to taking advice from, it will make the buying process easier for the business.

This principle is clear in an environment where you can predict your clientele. In a mass-market retail store environment you may witness a variety of customers. In this case, you dress in line with the role (manager, specialist, salesperson, hotel concierge) and your industry. To be safe in an unknown territory, salespeople should avoid either end of the spectrum of dressing and just dress neutrally. In most cases, this looks like a button-up shirt and business trousers with no coat or tie.

Quick tips for professional dress —

WOMEN

- Excessive jewellery should be avoided. Think simple and classy, not disco ball

- Hair should be neat, with no elaborate hair pieces.

- I know you feel like items of clothing can be dressed up and down, but there is a limit. Crocs, slippers and tights will always be casual.

- Make-up is nice, heavy make-up is distracting.

- Fingernails should not be so long that people begin nominating you for the *Guinness Book of Records*.

MEN

- Avoid any unnecessary jewellery. The most acceptable types of jewellery in the eyes of our customers are a wedding band and a watch.

- Always be clean-shaven. Thick beards can be a sign of aggression and short beards are best kept for the weekend, along with other passing trends.

- Your tie should have a knot appropriate to the cut of your shirt.

- Avoid stripes on stripes and checks on checks.

- Keep your tie darker than your shirt.

- The most professional shoes are the ones that do not get a reaction. Keep them neutral.

5 KEEPING THE CUSTOMER ENGAGED

THE MOST INTERESTING THING TO OUR CUSTOMERS

So often, organisations are out there selling their products through advertising, direct sales and mail-outs in the most disinteresting way. They are stereotypically telling us about an amazing offer, the deal of a lifetime and the incomparable features of their product. But who has told these companies that people even care about their products so much that they will be motivated to buy? These sales and marketing tactics should only ever expect to capture the attention of customers already interested in your product.

Believe it or not, the majority of your customers do not care about your products or your company, with the exception of cult-like brands such as Apple. Do you think that, if your organisation were to shut down tomorrow, your customers would see it as a life-changing experience? How quickly could they move on to your fiercest competitor? Even our most loyal customers care more about the characters of their favourite TV show than your products.

So if we want to get our customers' attention, let's talk about the most interesting thing to them—that is *themselves*! Each person is the platinum member of his or her own fan club. Our customers and the relevant benefits to them should be at the centre of all sales conversations. The moment you steer to a topic that is not about the customer, they become increasingly disengaged. Keep the customer engaged by making the conversation all about them. Tips on this will become clearer throughout this chapter!

VALUE IS SUBJECTIVE

The definition of the word 'value' in this context is the things that are important to the customer when making a buying decision. The topic of value often raises many debates among salespeople. On one side, some argue that the value of a product is objective as the price determines its worth, or that the end benefit, such as saving money and time, define the value of a product. The other school of thought is that it depends on the person's situation and how they will use the product or service.

To respond to this debate, imagine that we have conducted an experiment with a random group of people of different ages, nationalities and experiences. We hold up a basketball autographed by Michael Jordan and ask each individual in the group how much they think it is worth. What do you think the outcome will be? Will all of the individuals respond with the same price? Of course not. Some will be willing to pay in the thousands of dollars as they recognise this as a NBA fans' collector item, while others may not even know who Michael Jordan is and are happy to pay $10 as the basketball looks like it's useable.

How is it possible for a single product to have multiple prices? The product is identical for all potential buyers. Again, imagine if that same group were to be given an antique cabinet; again, the results will be similar, as some will perceive value and others will not. The reason for this inconsistency is simple—as Frank Romano, creator of *Precision Selling* once said, value is not objective; value is a perception. What *you* see as value-add in the products that you offer, others may not. Similarly, a customer may perceive value within a product that you don't. Value is purely a perception based on the customer's wants, needs, current situation and experiences. Even if the benefits of your product are monetary, value is still a perception; for example, your product or service could offer every customer a saving of one hundred dollars, which seems like a clear universal benefit. Yet one hundred dollars can mean different

72

things to different people. Some may quickly be motivated to buy, as one hundred dollars could clear a debt or buy their groceries, while others may feel that the inconvenience of shifting habits and using your products is more painful than the benefit of the money.

As salespeople, we can get caught up with our comprehensive product knowledge and personal experiences to the point where we begin to impose our values onto our customers. Don't mistake your situation for that of your customers. Avoid conversations that sound like, "This is my favourite part of the product." It's not only irrelevant; it is also an eye-rolling moment for the customer.

Your personal experiences and objections towards the product are specific to your needs and lifestyle. Unfortunately, customers don't care whether you like it or not. If you want to provide anecdotal evidence, share a customer testimonial from someone in a similar circumstance to them. Recently I went to buy a fruit and vegetable juicer and the salesperson was trying to steer me away from the one that I wanted as he felt it took up too much room in the cupboard. What he doesn't know is that I have one empty shelf in my cupboard that I wanted to dedicate to this juicer. The only thing that he achieved was raising doubt about a product that I was ready to buy.

The easiest trap that people fall into is objectifying the value of price. A telephone and Internet subscription salesperson I once met would deter customers from taking the highest package as they perceived it to be overpriced. Since he was protective of his money and values saving, he assumed that his customers were the same. This salesperson would always present the lowest-priced product in the hope of relating to customers' unknown desire to save. However, he lost many sales as customers valued internet speed over the additional money and would have been ready to purchase, until he steered them away. When selling on price, we should think about a waiter at a fine-dining restaurant trying to persuade someone to order Spam!

Projecting our own beliefs onto the customer is more common than we may assume. Think about the range of products you currently sell. Are there any items you rarely sell? Is there an option that you offer most of the time? Do you find yourself drawn to the easiest one to sell or the one that you are the most familiar with? Do these recommendations also correlate with the products that you own? If you answered yes to any of these, then you are selling based on your needs rather than those of your customers. To test this theory, I did some analysis with a company I was working with that sold a product offering nine different options. By 'options' I am referring to small, medium, large, or standard and premium. Recognising that the nine different options represented the nine different types of customers segments that they interacted with, I wanted to see whether one or two options were sold disproportionately more than others. Interestingly enough, over 40% of all sales were the cheapest option. You may think that this is because their customers were price-conscious. When we looked at the customers who cancelled their products, the primary reason was that they were not satisfied with the product. And the most successful retention strategy? Offering them a higher-tiered product. Customers whom we assumed wanted a cheap product stayed with the company only when offered something more expensive.

So if we know that value is a perception, how do we ensure that we are conveying the right value-adding message? We need to ask more questions.

IMPORTANCE OF QUESTIONS

Imagine how easy your job in sales would be if every customer you met proactively approached you and told you all of their wants, needs and preferences and how each of them correlated with the products and services that you had to offer. Well look no further, as that dream is possible—by asking the right questions. If we can nail the art of questions, we will not need to wait for the customer to spontaneously approach us. All we need to do is ask. Mastering this, will allow us to become incredibly influential in our personal and professional lives.

We know that questions are an important element of the sales process, but how important? I still hear sales people object to the notion of asking thorough set of questions, claiming that their spiel is powerful enough to convince people to buy. You may have heard comments such as, "if I already know what's right for the customer, then why continue asking questions?" and, "I can tell what the customer wants after asking one or two questions that I ask every customer," or, "I have the gift of the gab and convince people through my compelling arguments—no need to bother them with questions," or, "Why give customers the opportunity to interrupt my powerful presentation?"

True and long-lasting success in sales does not come from one person persuading another. This form of selling often leads to resentment as people feel like they were pushed into a decision. Our customers' minds will produce walls of resistance against anyone trying to control them or shape their thinking. We are all naturally sceptical towards this style of persuasion and our customers are no exception. Customers prefer to have conversations and want you to learn more about them so that they feel confident that they are making the right decisions.

Like education, the only way people are influenced is to arrive at an understanding themselves. Of course, questions alone will not close a sale; instead, they act as a guide to facilitate the path of buying that the customer is walking on. Questions help the salesperson guide the direction of the conversation and then allow the customer to create an outcome.

When you are speaking with a customer, they are continuously distracted by the various thoughts and memories floating around in the unconscious mind. The mind contains so much stimulus that it is unrealistic to expect the customer to give you their undivided attention and concentrate on every word you are saying. Questions are also the best technique to keep your customers engaged. When asked, questions can open up the customer's conscious mind and block out the unconscious in order for them to concentrate on delivering an answer. The more statements you replace with questions, the more engaged your customer will be.

QUESTIONS TO ALIGN PERCEPTIONS

If your customer has never used your product or service before, it is very difficult for them to appreciate its value. Presenting value in a clear way that aligns the customer's understanding to yours is a challenge in sales. How does someone gauge an appropriate price if they are unfamiliar with the product, haven't bought one before or have never used it? Answer: through comparison!

A great example of how we can demonstrate value through comparison is selling airline club lounges. Most airline lounges provide a comfortable waiting area, Internet connection, computers, printers, unlimited food/drinks and magazines to read.

Assuming you travel at least twice a month, how much is a reasonable price? $100 a year? $200? Some clubs charge over $500 for a 12-month membership— that sounds a bit steep, but what are we comparing it to? If we are comparing the lounge to sitting at the gate for free, then $500 is far too much to pay. On the other hand, if you compare it to the volume of overpriced airport meals you purchase for each return flight you take twice a month (48 single flights a year) divided by the price of the membership ($500), it will only cost $10.40 for unlimited meals and comfort each time you fly. This comparison suddenly demonstrates the value of this membership.

Ask compelling questions that allows the customer to articulate the difference between your product an alternative. This can lead them to the understanding of the value your product or service offers. In the airline lounge example, you may say,

"How many flights do you take each month/year? How often are you buying meals? If you don't mind me asking, what do those meals cost each time. Using your responses I will make a quick calculation to compare your current expenditure with the benefits and investment of joining our club"

Value comparison is not limited to price; it can also be used to highlight functionality benefits. If you are selling a car GPS, for example, you may compare the benefits of your product to the inconvenience of using a paper map, the embarrassment of asking for directions and the frustration of getting lost. A few hundred dollars seems minimal when comparing it with the alternative reality.

When you are trying to explain a product that a customer has not used before, don't just focus on them understanding the features of the product; remember that they are also calculating the value of the product when making a decision.

A GOOD QUESTION TO START WITH

You can have all of the best presentation skills in the world, but if the customer is not even eligible or able to buy your product, then you are just wasting their time and yours. One of the first questions that needs to be asked will be a qualifying question, through which you determine the eligibility of the customer. This question will be different for all products and customer types you are selling to; however, the principle is the same. Sometimes you may feel that your product is so simple it does not require prequalification, which is what my staff felt when I worked in the subscription television business. There were countless occasions where a salesperson would approach a customer and invest fifteen minutes in selling all of the features and benefits of pay-TV, only to learn that the customer does not own a television. Not own a television? Surely that's rare! Yes, it is. The Australian Communications and Media Authority have stated that approximately 100,000 Australian households do not have a functioning television, which represents 1.1% of homes. This turns out to be the equivalent of one customer a week for each salesperson. With eight salespeople not qualifying the customer appropriately, each member wasted 15 minutes, totalling to two hours of selling time a week. Asking a simple qualifying question like, "Do you have a television?" will save you time and maintain your professionalism.

What is your product and what are the bare basic requirements to qualify for these products? Is it affordability, age, postcode, residential status, occupation, credit history? Of course, some of these questions, such as affordability and credit history, can be delicate, so how do we ask these questions without offending the customer and losing rapport? We will explore this later on in this chapter.

MODERN HISTORY OF SALES

Humankind has been selling as long as it has had goods to offer, which one can imagine stretches back beyond recorded history. The history of sales entails many milestones, from its infancy in bartering for food and gold, to its childhood during the industrial revolution. Sales made its biggest shift when it evolved during its rebellious years of adolescence post-World War II, where riskier and more outward approaches were adopted, similar to what would be now seen as an aggressive form of door-to-door sales.

To truly understand this, let's take ourselves back to a beautiful sunny day in Chicago in the 1950s. You are sitting at home with your family. You might be cooking a meal, reading the paper or spitting tobacco on the floor. As you sit there in peace, you suddenly hear a cheery knock at the door. One of your children turns to you and says, "Hey, Ma, hey Pa! Someone's at the door!" Filled with deep interest and curiosity, your entire family rush to the door to see who it is. You open and the door and you see a gentleman in a pinstripe suit, holding a briefcase and a pile of visual aids, and sporting the cheesiest smile you have ever seen. This interesting character gives an energetic wave and yells out, "Well, howdy ya'll! Have I got a deal for you?" and quickly whips open his briefcase to show you a range of anything from steak knives to fridges with—yes you've guessed it—"a product with your name on it". This person will be speaking a hundred miles an hour with their foot in the door and not taking no for an answer!

What do you think you would have done in this situation? Told him you weren't interested? Asked him to leave? Slammed the door? Well, actually, if this was you in the 1950s, it is very likely that you would have done the complete opposite: you would have opened the door with great excitement and said, "A deal for me? Well, come on in." This may well have been the highlight of your day. This may have been the first time in your life that a complete stranger had appeared at your door offering you the latest and greatest deals. This method of selling was so successful in that era that Chevrolet used to sell cars door-to-door in the 1940-50s. Cars? Who on earth is buying vehicles on an impulse decision? Well, guess what—it worked.

So let's bring it back to today and imagine that you sitting at home watching a TV game show with your partner. Your kids are in their separate rooms surfing the Internet and it's getting dark outside, when all of a sudden you hear the sound of a pen tapping against your fly-screen door. The TV is now on mute and the family look confused and worried, wondering what someone would be doing approaching their home unannounced. Is it an emergency? Is there bad news? Are we being robbed? As you open the door with caution, you see a young adult in a ratty polo shirt with a faded logo, a pair of baggy jeans and a branded lanyard displaying the logo of an energy supply company. This salesperson opens their mouth to say, "Excuse me, sir, I can tell that you are paying too much on your electricity. Would you like me to show you..." *SLAM!* And the door is shut or at best you quickly slipped in "Not interested" and then double-locked your doors.

The market has changed. Our customers are savvier and we can no longer use 1950s tactics to get results today. Ask yourself, are your methods of engaging customers moving and evolving at the same pace of your customers? Are you frequently reflecting on the suitability of your conversation style based on a rapidly changing environment? Our clients are sensitive to poor and out-dated sales practises and will become disengaged at the slightest hint of it. Avoid staying comfortable and continuously develop your sales conversations.

MEMOIRS OF A CROSS-SELL ATTEMPT

When my wife and I moved into our new home, one of the most painful parts of the process was having to call the plethora of companies that I subscribe to or buy from to update my address details. Unknowingly, I opened myself up to a tsunami of sales attempts, which was a great opportunity to see how different companies train their staff to do this.

To be honest, I was underwhelmed by all of their attempts. None of them hit the mark and got me remotely interested in what they had to offer. They all gave me the same type of product-pushing spiel. I could just imagine them sitting in a call centre with all of these great one-liners laminated and sticky-taped to their computer monitors waiting for their vulnerable prey.

Throughout all of the seminars and coaching that I have been a part of, I hear people ask me what the most effective one-liners are or what scripts work best for me. Selling is a dynamic conversation that is not confined to a rigid script. If it was that simple, I would never have written a book. Capturing customers' attention and getting them interested in what you have to say requires an understanding on consumer behaviour. We need to first put ourselves in our customers' shoes and join their model of the world.

Imagine that you are calling up your insurance company, just to change your address. Think about what goes on in your mind as you wait on hold: "How long is this going to take?... I have better things to do with my time... what's for lunch?... These guys need to improve their hold music..." After being told that you have progressed in the queue, these thoughts begin to heighten until, like an oasis in a desert you hear, "Thank you for waiting. Can I start with your membership number?" You go through the ropes of

79

policy and procedure and let the customer service representative know that you need to change your address. They happily help you and just when you think you are off the hook, you hear, "When are you taking your next holiday?" or, "What do you do for a living?" or, "What would you do if you lost your job?"

Now pause. As the customer, what are you thinking right now? What internal questions are being asked? One would probably be thinking, "Why did she just ask me that? What's the relevance? Okay, here we go—what are you trying to sell me? I don't have time for this." We know that these internal thoughts go on in the customer's mind because the same thoughts fill our minds when the tables are turned. These so-called compelling one-liners are having the adverse effect and salespeople need an alternative.

We need to remember that our customers have gained a deeper understanding about what we do and how we do it. They know that we are incentivised, use leader boards, have sales training and that our customer service is being measured a post-interaction surveys. So if that is the case, then why do salespeople continue asking abrupt and ineffective questions? The most effective cross-sell lines are ones that answer those internal thoughts in the customer's mind: "Why are you are you asking me this? What's the relevance? What are you trying to sell me? I don't have time for this."

To cross-sell/up-sell/companion-sell is becoming more and more relevant in this highly competitive economy. As our companies' purse strings get tighter, the pressure to sell more has consequently increased. Our managers are telling us to add on extra products during every customer interaction—but they fail to educate us on how to integrate it into the conversation. So what usually happens? We end up product-flogging and abruptly asking, "Did you know about our low-rate credit card?" or, "While you're here, we can also give your car a polish" and, "We have a great promotion at the moment"—all of which sounds like, "Would you like fries with that?"

Since selling is merely a type of conversation, the root cause of these issues comes down to the way that we communicate in general. From childhood, we have become accustomed to starting with 'what' followed by 'why'; for example, when we wanted to influence our parents, we would blurt out what we wanted and follow it up with a justification. "I want to eat pizza (what), because

I'm hungry (why)," or, "Can I go to Andrew's party (what); all my friends are going (why)." We even do it as adults: "Let's go to the movies (what); it'll be fun (why)." We may have got away with this when we were children; however, it can get us into trouble when we slip into these habits in sales.

When we start with the '*what*', we are immediately revealing that we have an agenda and everything after that is a justification. Have you ever said something like this to a customer: "You should hear about our great product (what), which will save you lots of money (why)"? As mentioned previously, our customers are educated and far more sensitive to poor sales practice. All they will be thinking is, "You don't care whether I save money; you're just trying to sell me something."

So how do we cross-sell without just flogging the product? Can we ask a question that will not result in a customer's resistance or any other internal barrier? Yes—in fact, there are three key steps to linking to an effective cross-sale; *relevance*, *benefits* and *permission*. These steps move from the tradition '*what* → *why*' to a more modern '*why* → *how*'. They answer the thoughts of "Why are you are you asking me this?", "What's the relevance?", "What are you trying to sell me?" and, "I don't have time for this" before they enter the customer's mind. Let's explore *relevance*, *benefits* and *permission* in the following sections.

RELEVANCE

When our companies have a strong focus on a particular product or marketing campaign, we begin to forget about the customers' needs and start playing a numbers game: offer the deal/special to as many people as you can and then eventually, you'll get a yes. Sure, there are some plausible elements to this theory; that is, by chance eventually one person will be interested in what you have to say. However, in this competitive market, we cannot afford to burn a heap of customers just to promote an offer.

When we ask completely unrelated and generic questions to our customers in the name of a company-wide focus, they will be thinking, "I came to the pharmacy to pick up my prescription— why are you talking about an insole for my shoe?... Where is this coming from?" Asking seemingly irrelevant questions to get sales is like trying to stop strangers in the street asking for money. Yes, there are a lot of opportunities—however, it is hard. When we ask a relevant question, on the other hand, it is more like asking a friend for a favour: effortless and not intimidating.

The owner of a tea distributor, whom I have coached, attended a business course that took her through the many facets of running a business, and one of the course days was spent on sales. She asked the facilitator, "If I want a café to stock my tea, what are some of the best questions to ask the business owner?" The facilitator gave a variety of questions for her. She felt uncomfortable with some of the questions as they didn't make a lot of sense when she played them over in her mind. The main question that the coach insisted on her asking was, "What are your business priorities?" It seems like a great consultative question to learn about the café and where they are headed; however, from the perspective of a tea distributor, it seemed slightly irrelevant. Surely the café owner must be thinking, "Why on earth is a tea maker asking me about by business?" This would only be a good question in the 1% chance that the owner would say, "I am looking at expanding my hot beverage range," and then—*bang*—she could have jumped in with the best answer. However there is no way of guaranteeing what the answer will be. Even though you may be scripted at times, the customer is certainly not—conversations are dynamic and can move in any direction. Now let's imagine that the café owner responded to the *business priorities* question differently and said, "Fix my staff turnover issues" or, "Start a franchise" or, "Buy new equipment in the kitchen" or, "Start a Facebook page". A question as broad as 'What are your business priorities?' is not only irrelevant coming from a tea distributor, but has also wasted the customer's time and moved further away from helping them.

On the other hand, we have salespeople who ask questions that have a relevant basis; however, when delivered, sound completely irrelevant—for example, if someone was selling a credit card and asked the question, "How often do you travel?" it would seem completely irrelevant to customer. Whereas to the salesperson, this question is very relevant as that particular credit card has complimentary travel insurance or reduced international transaction fees. How is the customer supposed to know that? It is not fair to expect the customer to draw the link between your question and the hidden benefits of your product. Therefore, by not prepositioning our question, we have immediately moved the customer from curious to suspicious.

The great news is that if our question does have a relevant basis and the customer asks, "Why are you asking this?" we actually know the answer. That is because we have identified a trigger that prompted us to ask it in the first place. In the case of the tea salesperson, they may have walked into the café and identified that they only stock off-the-shelf tea bags, and many of their customers are the right target market for exotic teas. The salesperson would be eager to ask, "Can you tell me what kinds of customers visit your café?" To save the question from sounding irrelevant, all we need to do is reveal the reason we are asking the question. Essentially, we are answering the question, 'Why are you asking me this?' before the customer says it; for example, "I have noticed that you are currently using tea bags at the café. Which type of customers typically purchase these? Does this customer type match your typical customer base?"

By simply prepositioning your question with your honest observation, you keep your customer's mind free of distracting internal dialogue. Asking relevant questions may seem like an obvious point to make, however it is certainly not common practice. For some strange reason, salespeople feel the need to hide these triggers that they have identified, as if they are a salesperson's secret. They ask questions like a mysterious soothsayer and reveal the answer like a cheap magician. We no longer need to hide our thought process; rather, we should be completely transparent and tell the customer what the trigger was that we identified. The customer will appreciate the honesty and clarity. Sales should be a consultative conversation, not a magic trick. Sharing your relevant trigger can be as easy as starting a sentence with, "Based on what I can see…" or, "You mentioned to me that…" or, "Now that you are…"

If you are unsure whether the question is relevant, try and role-play with someone so they can step out of the detail and put themselves in the customer's frame of thinking. If this is not possible, ask the question to a customer and if the response is irrelevant to your proposed solution, then so was your question.

BENEFIT

Sudden questions can be intimidating to the customer as it's the first time in the sale that they are required to take ownership of the conversation's direction. Let's join our customer's model of the world and imagine that we are walking through a shopping centre, minding our own business and suddenly someone pops out in front of us and quickly asks, "How often do you wash your car?" On paper, this may seem like an innocent and harmless question—what harmful action could someone possibly perform with this information? Yet in reality, when it is asked, the prospective client puts up a force field of suspicion and thoughts. Even if the salesperson tries to make the question relevant by saying, "I can see that you are wearing a Toyota shirt—you must be into cars. How often do you wash your car?" it is still not enough. The customer will still be asking, "Who are you?", "Where are you from?", "Why do you want to know this?" and "Why should I answer this question?"

When introducing a new idea, product, service or concept into the conversation, the customer understands that they will need to invest more time and energy in speaking with you. So, why should they? What's in it for them? In a sales conversation, you are being paid to maintain rapport with the customer—they, on the other hand, have not committed to the same obligation with you. The customer can walk away at any time, so you must give a compelling reason for them to keep speaking with you. Since we live in a world that is governed by the law of reciprocity—that is, we need to give something in order to get something in return—then we cannot simply expect the customer to comply with our requests. If we expect to receive time and attention from our customer, what can we give them that can be seen as a fair trade?

If the customer is thinking, "Why should I answer this? What will I get out of it?" That's it! That is all you need to answer before the customer asks that question in their mind. If you can explain the benefit that you are leading to with your question, then you are almost guaranteed to get a response—as long as the benefit is relevant.

Remember, the customer does not care about your products alone. They care about the most important person in the world to them—themselves! So your benefit needs to be about them. For example, "There may be a way that we can save you some money" or, "There is an opportunity to make things more convenient for you,", as opposed to saying, "Our health plan will save you money"—this is the language of a commission-focused product flogger!

So, now that we know that cross selling or introducing product questions for the first time need be both relevant and beneficial to the customer, let's join them together: "I can see that you are wearing a Toyota shirt—you must be into cars (relevance). To be sure that I can save you money on the maintenance of your car (benefit)…" And then we need *permission*.

PERMISSION

Now that our questions are explicitly relevant to both the customer's situation and our solution and we have given the customer a reason to answer, due to our strong benefit, it's time to complete the process.

I am a firm believer that if a customer approaches you about a product or service, then you can be bold and beautiful and ask as many questions as you need. On the other hand, if you are about to introduce a topic that the customer has not asked about and may not be prepared to speak about, it can throw them off. Also, a great salesperson will always make sure that the customer feels in control of the conversation—and as soon as you ask an abrupt question, you are demonstrating control. In order to avoid customers not being ready for questions or agreeing to speak, we need to ask permission to ask the question. This technique will knock down the client's internal barriers to answer—for example, "Can I ask…" or, "May I ask…" or, "Let me ask you…"

Of course, asking permission to ask questions should not be seen as a passive symbol of a lack of confidence. Instead, it is a bold sign of humility that unconsciously satisfies the customer's need to stay in control.

An example of piecing the above three principles together: "Based on what I can see (relevance), there may be an opportunity to save you money (benefit). Can I ask (permission)…". This type of entry line does not mention the product or make a recommendation too early. The only thing that we are talking about is a potential benefit for the customer, to keep them engaged. To avoid sounding like a robot, customise these questions to your own products by using the principles of the *relevance, benefit* and *permission*, rather than scripting it. Getting clear responses that lead to sales outcomes will be easier for you and your customers will appreciate the difference.

SELL THE CONVERSATION, NOT THE PRODUCT

One of the misconceptions around connecting questions, transition lines or conversation segues are that they are designed to sell the product. Instead, they should be used to sell the conversation. The 'relevance, benefit and permission' approach sells the idea of spending more time with you. Remember, every 30 seconds buys you the next 30 seconds. The crucial part is to excite the customer about the possibility of a benefit, introducing the product later. These entry lines into the questioning process allows you to gauge the relevant benefits for the customer. There is no use in promoting a product that offers a benefit that the customer is not interested in.

VALIDATING IDENTITY

People will always act consistent with their perception of their identity. If they see themselves as a good person, they act on this and lead with morality. If someone believes that they are lazy, they will be the first to bail on an activity. It might seem like we are mixing up cause and effect here and ignoring the fact that people can be good and lazy and that's what they believe. However, behaviour and self-belief act cyclically and thus feed into each other. From a salesperson's perspective it is useful to recognise the relationship between identity and action so we can influence buying behaviour by validating the identity of the customer.

In your process of discovering what is important to the customer, you will surely learn a little bit about how they perceive themselves. You will gauge whether they are decision-makers, powerful, timid/weak, determined, collaborative, honest and/or friendly. When recognising these qualities, we can use them as a reminder to the customer and as a way to align our offering.

You may say, for example, "I can see that you are someone who appreciates good quality, which is why…" or, "From what you have told me, you make wise decisions in the best interest of your family. This is why I want to show you…" Once you have validated that identity, the customer, like any other human being, will commit their actions to that belief. Ensure that the identity that you are validating is an encouraging one and your comments will serve as positively reinforcing affirmations. You do not want to say, "Sir I can see that you are very lazy, which is why I know you will watch this TV every day." When the customer can relate to your products, the buying decision becomes a lot easier.

CAN THERE BE TOO MANY QUESTIONS?

Yes. If you find that you are asking too many, it can either mean that you are having to ask too many closed questions or that you are not asking relevant/targeted questions to gain the desired response from the customer. It helps to write down, word for word, the questions that you generally ask, and assess whether they are necessary to you leading to the right outcome for the customer, then decide whether or not it could be reworded to gather better responses. If you struggle with determining the quality of your questions, practice them with a colleague/coach/manager or a friend who may not know much about your product or company who can share their thoughts and insights.

KEEP IT SIMPLE

One of the world's leading marketing agencies, M&C Saatchi, make a truthful statement as a part of their brand philosophy: 'It's easier to complicate than simplify.' Salespeople often fall into this trap. When we communicate with the customer, we have all of these ideas and potential things to say and key selling points; however, maybe the customers want to know a lot less than that. This is not because your customers are not intelligent; it's because they do not buy products for every single feature or benefit. Remember, selling is a conversation, not a product training, so let's keep it simple.

Below are a few quick tips to keeping it simple:

- Customers love choice, but hate too many options

- Customers want the facts, but will avoid detail

- What is simple to you can be complicated to others

- Be super clear but not patronising

- Educate through a logical structure, but do not be too rigid

- Remember people buy the *why* not the *what*

If you can find the balance between both sides of the spectrum, you have an interesting and simple message.

STATISTICS AND SOCIAL PROOF

A professional salesperson must possess a memory bank of valuable statistics that work as proof points to their passion and anecdotal claims. Social proofing, which is the evidence created based on the behaviour of a population, has always been a powerful tool to generate interest in products or services. This does not only apply to the world of sales, as social proofing also helps us decide what we click on when we are surfing the Internet. Have you ever browsed on YouTube and then clicked on a video because it had a lot of views, or wanted to read the article in the news that was the most trending? Restaurants are now chosen based on people's subjective online reviews and people.

I see social proofing at its finest every day when I walk through the city and stand at a traffic light waiting for the flashing green man signalling me to walk across the road. Unlike me, not everyone shares my patience and I typically witness an eager jaywalker ready to make their move and staring down each end of the intersection to see if it's safe to go. When there is no sign of oncoming cars, the jaywalker dashes across the street. So what are the other pedestrians doing? Despite the risk of being run over by a car, people are not looking for oncoming cars as an indicator to cross the road. Instead, they are keenly observing the original jaywalker—if he moves, they follow. Even in a high-risk situation, people are comfortable to follow the opinion of complete strangers. This is the power of social proof.

In the book *Influence, the Psychology of Persuasion* Robert Cialdini demonstrates how the size of the crowd can impact the level of influence. Think about watching a comedy movie by yourself; there will only be a few outrageously hilarious moments where you will laugh out loud. Now imagine watching that same movie in a room full of your friends and they are laughing throughout the movie— aren't you likely to laugh at more moments? Now imagine you are in a stadium at a comedy show; why is that you laugh at almost every joke? The more people perform a behaviour, the more socially acceptable it becomes.

Social proofing through statistics and testimonials becomes a powerful sales tool, as they demonstrate how buying your product is a socially acceptable norm. Your previous customers indirectly become your salespeople. We should be proud to use testimonials to inspire belief in the customer and allow them to understand the value of the product or service from a different perspective.

Sharing statistics that indicate success, product use, popularity and feedback are influential and very difficult to object to. One can always challenge your opinion on the product; however, one cannot simply argue with facts and statistics. The fact that five million people have purchased this product in the last 12 months, or the fact that the product generates over one thousand dollars of value, or that the customer saves an average of four hundred dollars per year, makes your sales presentation very compelling.

Almost every company has these powerful statistics somewhere. Often, statistics are held in safekeeping in Head Office and are not being used to arm the frontline. Find them, analyse them and unleash them.

LOGIC AND FEELING

In order to remain interesting in the game of sales, do we need to stimulate the minds of our customers or their emotions—which is more powerful? As you would have predicted, the answer is *both are powerful*. Brian Tracy in his bestselling book *Psychology of Selling*, shares that we use logic to justify our emotional buying decisions; therefore, neither logic nor emotion are powerful on their own— they should always be used together. If you try and reach out to the customer through logical reasoning alone, you may only give them enough information to continue doing their homework and seek out competitors' offers. On the other hand, if you only excite people into the sale through emotion, you are likely to make the initial sale, which will be followed by either a cancellation, refund or customer dissatisfaction as all of the objections that would have been handled at the point of sale came to the customer's mind post-purchase.

VISUAL, VOCAL, VERBAL

Conventional sales practice preaches that a good salesperson needs to have the gift of the gab and a way with words. Well, this is only one part of the story. In the art of communication, words are powerful; however, they do not function effectively on their own. Words provide the content and the logic—but customers' buying behaviours are not only based on logic. Consumers also make purchasing decisions with emotion. As such, to be more compelling in a sales conversation, we need to show emotion through the tone of our voice, our body language and the expressions on our face.

As discussed in the chapter on Sales Mindset, your own belief towards your product, the customer's best interest and your organisation are important elements of success. However, it is one thing to be passionate about what we are selling, and it's another thing to show the customer our passion through effective one-to-one communication.

Albert Mehrabian, a renowned professor at UCLA, conducted an experiment on communication to learn more about the relationship between the meaning of words, tone of voice and non-verbal communication. These different types of communication are more widely known as the '3 V's of Communication': visual, vocal and verbal. His experiment had a specific purpose and it was not primarily around sales; however, we can apply the principles of his findings in the context of keeping the customer engaged.

Mehrabian's experiment drew fascinating insights on how emotion is communicated. He uncovered that 55% of the feelings behind the overall message came from visual communication: facial expressions, body language and visual cues. This is no surprise considering that the amount of nerves connecting the eye to the brain is estimated as being 22 times the amount going from the ear to the brain. Vocal communication, which refers to the tone, pitch and rate of our speech, attributed to 38% of the emotion that was communicated. Which leaves only 7% for verbal—the actual words that we say. This of course does not conclude that words are not important, as they are critical in communicating the key elements of the message. Rather, Mehrabian's study highlights how visual and vocal communication can enhance your conversations with your customers by communicating attitudes and feelings towards the words that are being said.

VISUAL COMMUNICATION

Let's explore some visual communication that may move beyond the initial findings or purpose of Mehrabian's research. The first principle of visual communication is congruency: the alignment of your verbals and your non-verbals. Verbally, I could easily say to the customer that I am very excited to be speaking to them about this product; however, if my back is slouched over, my eye contact is poor, my head is down or I am leaning back in my chair, I am communicating a very different story. Remember; by explaining my emotion through words alone, no matter how I genuinely feel, my words will only attribute to 7% of the buying emotion. The visuals need to be aligned.

We can also create trust by demonstrating congruency through the clothes that we choose to wear. For instance, if you met a real estate agent and she said, "I am a professional salesperson. I can guarantee the best price for your house," and she is wearing sweatpants and slippers, it would be very hard for you to believe her. Personal appearance is a highly underrated skill in sales. As a salesperson, you should have the discipline to look in the mirror every day before you go to work and ask, "Is the way that I dress and present myself aligned with the image of my role, organisation and customer's expectations?"

Visual communication is also critical to the educational process that you are undertaking with the customer. In an initial meeting with your customer, it is quite a challenge to discover whether the customer is a visual, auditory or kinaesthetic learner. To compensate for this lack of knowledge, therefore, we use all of them. Visual communications are quite powerful for most customers, and using brochures, digital sales tools, drawings and posters will always enhance the conversation that you have with your customers. Visual tools should be engaging and interactive and do not always have to be over the top. I know that when I speak with sales managers and salespeople, as soon as I say *visual tool*, they think tablets (e.g., iPads) and large-screen TVs. This is not always the case, as these tools, although fun and interactive, can sometimes be a distraction. One organisation I was working with had over 396 outlets across the country and simply couldn't afford to purchase a tablet for each staff member across all stores, so instead we explored what the intended purpose of the tablets were. What they actually wanted them for was to simplify complicated products and options for the customer. This did not need to be achieved through tablet apps or websites, instead the art of drawing steps/stages/options could achieve the same end. So, instead of buying expensive tablets, we purchased nine-dollar A4-size whiteboards on which each staff member could use to draw complicated options for the customer. This simple tool, based on a real diagnosis, was a huge hit for this company and is now formally adopted across all stores. It has increased confidence in selling higher tier products and discussing complex matters that previously ended in awkward conversations.

DRAW WITH YOUR WORDS

In circumstances where you are selling over the phone or do not have the product/service to demonstrate in front of the customer, you are often left with your words to paint a picture for the customer. So how clear are you? Of course, we all sound crystal clear to ourselves, but are the explanations of our products following a logical sequence and are we speaking in a way that an uninformed bystander could understand?

As discussed in the previous chapter, using our words and tones alone makes the communication process more challenging—so we need to get good at it. So how good are we at verbally and vocally communicating concepts? Here is a test that my first sales mentor did with me that I never forgot.

STEP 1

Draw five random shapes on a piece of paper and do not show anyone. Make sure they are randomly placed, instead of all sitting next to each other.

STEP 2

Ask someone who you do not speak to on a regular basis to sit in a room with a pen and paper.

STEP 3

Facing your backs to one another and using your words alone, try to explain the drawing and ask the other participant to draw what you explain. Take as long as you need. Remember, they have never seen the shapes and cannot see your facial expressions and hand gestures. The other participant is not able to ask you questions, just draw what you tell them to.

STEP 4

Once you feel that you have explained enough, sit the two drawings next to each other and see how similar they are. Then ask the other participant how clear they felt you were, and if there were differences between the drawings, ask them why they thought that is what you meant.

You will gain many insights into the way you communicate in general, which is a skill that goes beyond the desire of getting sales. Like many sales competencies, communication is also a fundamental life skill.

INVOLVE THE CUSTOMER

As the Chinese proverb states, "Tell me, I'll forget. Show me, I'll remember. Involve me, I'll understand." This teaching philosophy provides great insight into the sales process.

The most powerful visual and kinaesthetic tool is the product itself. If your product or service is such that one can be see, hear, touch and use, then we need to give that experience to the customer. How many of us would buy a car without test-driving it? In Israel, felafel stores attract people in by having fresh felafels served for customers to taste-test before they buy. This puts a distinct taste in customers' mouths that needs to be satisfied by eating the entire meal. The greatest of all product demonstrations is performed at pet stores. If you are interested in a dog or cat, for example, they will let you buy it and try it out for a week. If you are unsatisfied, you can return the animal. Of course, this very rarely happens as families fall in love with the pet and could not stomach the idea of returning it. How much more compelling are these demonstrations than the most well-articulated words in a sales presentation?

Customers will be far more likely to buy once they have used your product and begun imagining it in their life.

IT'S NOT ALL ABOUT PRICE

A family-run barbershop that has been operating for over 20 years is well known to the locals for their good haircuts, great service and fair prices—which is and has always been $25 per cut. One day, a new barbershop opens right across from them and they place a big sign in the window saying '$6 haircuts'. The barber thinks to himself, "How can I compete with this? If I lower my price to $6, I will go broke and have to shut down the shop." The barber thinks hard, and the next day he places a large sign in his front window that says, "WE FIX $6 HAIRCUTS".

The purpose of this anecdote is that we can combat aggressive price strategies without lowering our own price. In my experience, I have seen salespeople become price-obsessed and see it as the be-all and end-all of the sale—that is, if the competition offers a lower price, then it's time to give up. Within the context of an unpredictable and unstable market, we develop perceptions about the customer's elasticity towards price and how it affects their desire towards purchasing our products and services. Companies have become very reactive to this perception and use price as their way to attract customers and win their business. This mindset is a trap and one that is difficult to escape from.

Recently, my wife and I went to buy a new couch from a trendy furniture store. We approached one of the salespeople and asked, "Can you please tell us about this couch?" As she heard the question, she sprung up from her chair and moved towards us and said, "The best price I can do is $9800 and if you can wait till next week, these couches are going on sale until February and they will be 50% off." If you haven't heard of this technique before, this is called *sandbagging*; when a salesperson holds off the potential sale or possible rejection in the hope to convince you over an upcoming deal.

There are a few problems with this technique:

1. Firstly, without even knowing about the discount, we were willing to purchase the couch at full price;

2. We do not go shopping for furniture on a weekly basis so it is unlikely that we will go back;

3. The couch has been devalued in our eyes and,

4. Most importantly, we never even asked about the price.

The salesperson must have held a personal belief that these couches are overpriced and used her perception to influence us. Unfortunately for the salesperson, it is only the perception of my wife and I that will determine whether we buy or not.

Salespeople are often sadly mistaken when it comes to their knowledge of buying behaviour and how customers respond to price. In Robert Cialdini's book *Influence: the Psychology of Persuasion*, he shares the story of a friend who owned an Indian jewellery store in Arizona who was struggling to sell a series of turquoise items. These items were of good quality and a fair price. She tried many tactics to draw attention to them in the hope that people would buy. In a rush to leave on a trip out of town, she writes a note to her salesperson saying, "Everything in this display case, price x ½" in a desperate hope to get rid of each item, even if it is at a loss. Those who feel price is a big determinant of the buying decision would agree that displaying the items at half price is a good strategy for selling the jewellery. In a misunderstanding of the note, the salesperson thought that the message said to multiply the price of each product by two instead of halve it. Of course, this would lead to a sales disaster—right? Wrong. The opposite happened: people who came and visited the store saw the high-priced jewellery and associated a high level of quality with it. By the time the owner came back from holidays, the entire allotment of turquoise had been sold.

We are more obsessed with price than our customers are. If your product was the cheapest in the market, do you honestly think that your low price would be the winning feature that makes your product more appealing comparatively to your competitors? Additionally, is continuously lowering your price the most sustainable approach? You may attract customers in the initial price drop or discount, but eventually you will push your prices so low that there is nowhere to go.

Think like the barber: let's stop lowering our price and let's raise our value. Show off the wow factors of your products and services that make your brand unique. Remind customers that going in and repairing or replacing a cheap alternative can cost you more than the one-off payment of your products. A bad product will cost you more in the long run than the initial payment for a high-quality good. Think of your own experiences about regretting the cheaper option. If we think it is easier to sell on low price, then think again. Would you risk a $6 haircut?

KNOW YOUR WOW FACTORS

If you want to raise your value while maintaining your price, you need to have a firm understanding of what you do that your competitors do not do. For the majority of us, we are selling products that our customers have heard of before; therefore, there is no need to spend too much time on the features that everyone else is talking about. Is there something that differentiates the quality of your products, the brand, the post-purchase service or the design? In many circumstances, your wow factors are the simple things that you do for free, like gift-wrapping, tailoring, advice, exceptional service and giving time.

In order to really appreciate the value of what you offer, you need take a walk and mystery-shop other businesses. Learn about how they sell, what they offer and what features they promote. If you do not understand your competitors, then how can you possibly compete?

Think hard. What differentiates your brand?

6 MAKING RECOMMENDATIONS

We have now walked into work with the right mindset, we have accepted that we are a player in the meaningful game of sales. This does not shape who we are; rather, it is an action we perform at work. We have built robust connections with our customers in order for them to like us, respect us and believe in what we say. We have captured the customers' attention by being interested and involving the customer in a conversation that they care about. We have invested the time to asking questions to uncover the customer's known and unknown needs. We are only now ready to make a recommendation.

Making a recommendation should be an easy process, particularly if we have done all of the above correctly. If we are not careful in demonstrating our products in a compelling and relevant way, then we are at risk of losing the customer and depriving them of a benefit that we know they need.

WHY SHOULD THE CUSTOMER BELIEVE YOU?

As we have previously explored, asking an ample amount of questions will build your confidence in making the right recommendation to the customer. Despite your confidence, the customer will need a little more before they truly believe that your offer is the right one for them. Below are some tips to help your customer believe in your recommendations:

CUSTOMISE—DON'T GENERALISE

Remember that there is a difference between the product and what the product will do for the customer. So often I hear rehearsed product explanations that aim to create a one-size-fits-all approach to selling. Customers will subconsciously switch off at any sight of a generic and rehearsed spiel about the product. Enduring salespeople have conversations, not presentations.

Do not disregard all of the time invested in asking questions and learning about the customer. At this stage, you would have accumulated a lot of crucial information about the customer. Use it and customise your recommendation directly to their needs. There is a distinct difference between, "This product will save you one hundred dollars" and, "Based on your current spending of $245 a month and your current financial circumstances, I can see how this product will save you a minimum of $100 a month." If you are selling mobile phone plans, you can say "To stay in touch with your family overseas and stay within your budget, I recommend…"

CONVICTION

Within the first few words, it will become very clear to the customer if you have conviction in your recommendation and believe in the product. If you don't believe that this product/service will benefit the customer, you are dreaming if you think there is a chance that they will. The solution: either don't make recommendations that you don't believe in or, if you don't believe due to personal opinions, study the facts and change your internal story.

BE OBJECTIVE

Nobody has more of an opinion of your company's offerings than you do; unfortunately, the majority of your customers do not care to hear them. Most of the time when they ask for your opinion, what they really want is your professional advice. Your thoughts and feelings do not play a role in their decision-making process.

Ensure that when you are promoting the features and benefits of your products, you are speaking about objective facts and not subjective opinions and claims. There is nothing more compelling and believable than a series of real facts—whether it be displayed in the form of a demonstration, a set of statistics or a fact sheet, it will still pack a punch. Think about the TV show *MythBusters*; it is a show where they road-test commonly known opinions and urban legends to prove whether they are facts or myths. To do this, the hosts of the show do not just sit and have a discussion on what they think of the claim or give vague opinions. Instead, they conduct experiments to prove their point.

Using facts as a way to influence may be obvious in the world of science, so let's think of a field similar to sales where influence is dependent on the individual: politics. How would your mind respond to the politician who claims, "My opinion tells me that taxpayers will be financially better off when my party is elected."? Your curious and responsible mind may be thinking, who cares about your opinion; if you are going to save me money, how will you do it, how much money will I save, by when, and what do we need to sacrifice to gain the extra benefit? Stick to the inarguable facts and your customers will readily believe.

OUR OPINION VS. THE CUSTOMER'S

As we know, people love to buy—but they hate to be sold to. When we are making recommendations to the customer, therefore, we need to be mindful of how we position it. The recommendation should not be seen as you forcing your personal or professional opinion on the customer—this will make the customer feel disempowered in the decision-making process or, worse, manipulated. Starting your sentence with, "In my professional opinion…" is in fact unprofessional as the customer does not care about your opinion. You do not have to live with the purchasing decision—they do. The only opinion that matters to people is their own. How many times in life do you hear people ask you leading questions that they want you to give them a specific answer to that satisfies their ego or validates their point of view? For example, "do I look nice?" People only ask this, because they think they look nice and they want you to agree—they don't want your opinion.

Instead of recommending products starting with, "I think you should..." we need to be clear that our suggestions are solely based on what the customer has already decided. You could say, "Mr Customer, you mentioned that you were looking for XY and Z, which is why this solution will suit your needs" or, "Based on what you have told me, it sounds like this will be perfect for you" or, "Knowing that your favourite flavour is red, let's take a look at our red option." Despite this being your recommendation, it is clear that it is the customer's recommendation.

WORDS CAN HURT

As a young child, I distinctly remember a time at school where a close friend was being bullied and someone called him a nerd. Not the harshest thing to say; however, the humiliation deeply hurt him and he ran to our teacher crying. The teacher asked him what was wrong and he explained that some of the other children had called him names, to which the teacher responded with this piece of advice that many of us have received in the past: "Sticks and stones can break your bones, but words can never hurt you." As a child, I used to think that this was great advice, despite the fact that it did not stop my friend from crying.

The older I got, the I realised how that was possibly some of the worst advice that the teacher could have given us. What a lie! If words could never hurt you, then why did he cry when he was called a nerd? Words are very powerful. Imagine if I took my wife out on a romantic date—the dinner was perfect, the weather was right, we stood facing a scenic view and I held her hands, looked deeply into her eyes and said, "I hate you." Let's just say that if that story were true, I would not be alive to write this book. On the contrary, imagine if I took her on the same date and said, "I love and adore you." Words are powerful.

Words also shape the way we perceive reality. A successful outsourced call centre in Australia found the power with words when they revolutionised the calibre and attitude of their front-desk receptionist, simply by changing the employee's title from *Receptionist* to *Director of First Impressions*. The next day, they saw not only the employee's outfit change, but her behaviour and total outlook about her role. The words that we use can even impact the way that we see ourselves. If you are salesperson who wishes to maintain their integrity, what impact would it have on you if you were to refer to customers as *idiots* or call the act of helping someone "smashing in a sale" or referring to your line of work as a 'cut-throat business'? Our perceptions are often limited by our abilities to express ourselves.

A salesperson at the Apple Store was once so particular about his words that he went out of his way to correct mine when I asked questions. When he finished explaining the features of their desktop computer, the iMac, I asked, "So how much will this cost me?" to which he sharply responded, "This is not a cost—it's an investment. And you would be investing $2199."

Words are powerful and the smallest error in language can sometimes be the end of the sale if we are not careful. Here is a list of words and the effective alternative:

WORDS THAT HURT	EFFECTIVE ALTERNATIVE
Sign up	Join us or become a member
Cost or pay	Investment
Contract	Agreement or plan
I don't know	That's an important question. Let me find the best answer for you
Hard or difficult	Stepping stone or exciting opportunity
I'll ask my manager	I would be delighted to find the answer for you

BENEFITS AND FEATURE EXTENSIONS

Most salespeople have a good theoretical grasp over the difference between a feature and a benefit; that is, features can simply be defined as the *things that the product does* and benefits are *what the customer gets out of it*. This understanding is correct; however, it is important to dig deeper so we never accidentally mix them up.

In a coaching conversation with a car salesperson, I asked him to give me an example of one of the features of a car and he said, "Air conditioning," which is correct. Then I asked him to give me the benefit of air conditioning and he said, "It makes sure the car stays cool on a hot day." Keeping the car cool—is that a feature or a benefit? Isn't keeping the car and the passengers at a fixed temperature in the car a basic function of air conditioning? It is very easy to fall into the trap of going only one layer in and thinking that this is a benefit. Many times I have heard a benefit being defined as the feature behind the feature. In fact, it is simply the benefit behind the feature. Therefore, 'staying cool' is just an extension of the feature of air conditioning. Think a few layers deeper, why does someone want air conditioning—to stay cool. Why does someone want to stay cool? What is that underlying feeling or emotion that will influence the buying decision? To be comfortable, perhaps. The benefit, therefore, is *comfort*. The intangible reasons are why customers make decisions and customers are motivated by these core generic benefits as they are easier to relate to and understand.

Let's break it down to a simpler example to ensure the principle is apparent. What is the feature of a pencil? It is made of wood, it is 12 centimetres long, there is a long piece of led in the middle of the wood and a coating of colour on the outside. Going one level deeper, we know that the pencil can write, draw and shade (extensions of the feature). A deeper feature extension of this product is that it allows one to express oneself, reflect and relax. So why does someone want to do either of those things? To feel peaceful? Perhaps—and you will easily discover this through strong questions and can then apply it immediately. If you want to be the most compelling pencil salesperson in the world, you should make recommendations that sound like this: "Mr Customer, to guarantee the most peaceful experience when creating art, there is a pencil that is comfortable to hold and allows your fingers to move at the same rate as your imagination."

BENEFITS CAN BE MORE THAN JUST THE GOOD STUFF

According to the dictionary, the word *benefit* is defined as, "An advantage or profit gained from something." Therefore if human beings are driven by incentives, we can then infer that benefits direct decisions and influence behaviour. Benefits make us change our minds, view things differently, act and not act upon something in the hope it will lead us towards somewhere better. We are all seekers of pleasure; however, life experience tells us that there is more to this story as many decisions are driven by things that do not lead to a form of pleasure. When I was learning sales, I was always taught to only focus on the pleasures that are gained from the use of the products and services, and I therefore failed to see other motivating factors that may have propelled them to make such a choice. There are times when customers are more motivated by *not* moving forward as a way to protect the status quo or avoid the risk of a worse outcome.

We see motivation to act/buy as multifaceted and recognise that our unconscious mind and nervous system are hardwired to seek out pleasure and avoid pain. It is for this reason that we can understand why people are not motivated to go to the dentist. Very few people feel an overwhelming sense of excitement when thinking about what they will receive from the dentist, even in circumstances when they are currently in pain. We do not go to the dentist to gain pleasure; instead, we go there to avoid future pain.

It would be superficial to think that benefits are only limited to the positive outcomes derived from an act, as a benefit is also about avoiding pain. To put it simply, in life, every behaviour and decision is motivated by two things: to gain pleasure or to avoid pain—which, for the sake of this exploration, we will refer to as *benefits*. This notion is of course not an original idea and many readers will be familiar with this concept. Relating this to the game of sales, however, is where it becomes quite powerful. Knowing what motivates people to make decisions will assist you in relating to your customers in a way that shifts their thinking and draws them closer to understanding the benefits of your product.

A person's motivation between pleasure and pain is determined by both the individual's circumstances and values. Almost every product/service or decision can provide a pleasure and a pain; for example, buying a car could bring the pleasure of luxury and convenience, and also avoid the pain of using public transport or the embarrassment of asking people for a ride. When someone buys a camera, it could be to bask in the pleasure of capturing treasured moments and, through some people's perspectives, it could be to avoid the pain of missing a moment. We need to be conscious of these dual realities when asking the customer questions. If we fail to uncover the pain or pleasure that could determine whether the customer buys or doesn't buy, then our recommendations will be weak.

MITIGATING CHANGE

Conservative customers often fear change. They do not like a change in routine or having to learn new things. For these customers, we should avoid dramatic language when describing the impacts of our products. They don't like to hear that your product will change their life or revolutionise the way they do things. These customers respond more to improvements and enhancements rather than transformational benefits.

Show these customers how your products will improve their current situation by making it faster, cheaper and more effective.

SIX HUMAN NEEDS

Many of us will have studied or been exposed to Maslow's Hierarchy of Needs, which is a theory to describe the different human motivators and requirements for living, broken down into needs: physiological, safety, love/belonging, esteem and self-actualisation. There are some great truths in Maslow's theory, however it is too high-level and not helpful to direct our sales conversations.

On the other hand, Anthony Robbins, the world-renowned speaker, success coach, author and all-round genius, shared, in his book *Awaken the Giant Within*, the fact that humans have six basic needs. These needs are at a deeper level than Maslow's and help us position our products and services in a logical way that relates to the customer's wants and needs. These six needs are: certainty, uncertainty, significance, connection, growth and contribution. We naturally prioritise our needs as some resonate stronger than others; however, each one can apply to different situations. As you read the following paragraphs, consider which needs your customers value the most and which of these your products meet in the most compelling way.

CERTAINTY

The need for certainty is related to the comfort of knowing what is coming next and that you can trust things to happen the way you planned. This need is relevant to people who buy from you. In a sales presentation, we might spend time showing the customer all of the bells and whistles; however, primarily the customer needs to know if the product works and will perform its main function. It is all well and good that a vacuum cleaner comes with 37 different nozzles—instead, the prospect wants to be certain that it won't break down and that when they vacuum, it will pick up all of the dust. Simple! Don't forget some of the basics.

You can also leverage the need for certainty by managing the customer's expectation. Telling those who need certainty that their vacuum cleaner will arrive within five and eight days creates unnecessary angst. Instead, you need to tell them that it will arrive within eight days—and if it arrives earlier, then you will call them.

Robbins describes that eventually one becomes bored of certainty and needs some...

UNCERTAINTY

We all have a need for variety, spontaneity and feeling different. Customers like to be wowed and surprised, and know that using your product will not be the same over a long period of time. If you are selling a mobile phone, for example, sharing that from time to time there will be software updates and that new apps are being developed every day can add an element of excitement that things will improve and their experience with the product will not be boring.

SIGNIFICANCE

This need relates to the desire to feel important and special. If you are selling a holiday, you should be sharing with the customer how they will be treated by airline and hotel staff throughout the process. If they are being picked up from the airport, let them know that a chauffeur will be waiting for them. If the currency conversion is strong, remind them how rich they will feel when they go shopping in that country.

When someone is buying formal office attire, they want to know that they look important and professional or that they will stand out. I met a credit card salesperson who makes customers feel significant when he sells a premium card. He reminds his clients of the feeling that his other customers have shared when they pull a black shiny card out of their wallet to pay for dinner, which gets people asking questions.

This need does not only get satisfied through the benefits of your product, but must also be consistent throughout your conversation with the customer. If this is a dominant need of the customer, ensure that you share with them that their comments and opinions are valued. Show extra interest in their questions and never interrupt them—even out of excitement. Let them guide part of the conversation and be consultative in your approach.

CONNECTION

The need for connection is the need to give and receive love. This need can be fulfilled when people are buying gifts for others. When someone is browsing for another person, particularly someone they love, it can be difficult to make a decision, as they want it to be the right gift. We should not only remind them how much the recipient will love the gift, but also how much they will love the person who bought it for them. Of course, we don't need to go all Oprah on people; however, we should not neglect to mention, 'Yes, they will love you for it.'

GROW

Does your product allow others to grow financially or spiritually, or to develop intellectually? People have a strong desire to know that they are progressing and moving forward—despite the demon in all of us that loves to procrastinate. An obvious benefit that many of our products and services can achieve is the idea of saving or making money. Share how this can benefit the individual in the long term.

If you are selling an e-book reader, of course we want to cover the need of certainty and ensure the customer that the books they like to read will be available and that the device has a strong battery life. You can also demonstrate uncertainty, by showing the prospect the amount of categories of books available to download and how regularly they update. The customer can also feel significant, knowing that your e-reader carries a sense of prestige and that they will be at the cutting edge of innovation and style. Finally, you can remind the customer of the intellectual growth potential of having access to a database full of great learning and profound literature where they can explore new depths of imagination through exciting novels, or advance in their careers by reading skills-based books such as this one!

CONTRIBUTE

Humans have a fundamental need and desire to contribute, to give to others, to share and know that their achievements are benefiting the greater good. Can your product or service facilitate this? Can you give the customer the ability to give to others? Charities are trained well in leveraging this need, as the link to contribution is obvious; however, this is not exclusive to heroic deeds. People receive joy if they know that what they buy can be shared with others and make others happy. Even if we were to move far from philanthropic deeds and think about how buying a big TV with all of the specs can fulfil the need to contribute. This TV can bring about joy by bringing people together to watch movies and laugh together.

One of my favourite parts of reading books is to rush to my wife and tell her something interesting that I've learnt, or to meet some creative thinkers and contribute case studies that I have read in other business books.

One thing to remain conscious of is that your commission and well-being do not count for eliciting a contribution from the customer—trust me! A salesperson who used to work in my door-to-door business used to tell a plea story about the fact that he is paying his way through university by selling subscription television. Don't get me wrong; he wasn't lying and it did work from time to time—however, it very often resulted in cancellations as the commission of a salesperson is not a long-standing motivator for a customer, and buyer's remorse kicks in soon after.

COST AND SAVINGS

Now we know that words are powerful and that people are influenced by avoiding pain, we can use these lessons together when making recommendations to our customers. In Zig Ziglar's *Closing the Sale,* he uses these principals when selling the benefit of cost-saving to a customer. Ziglar encourages his readers to shift their perceptions away from the pleasure of saving money and to focus on the potential money lost if they were not to make the decision; for example, if a certain item saves the customer a dollar a day, it therefore is costing them a dollar each day that they decide not to buy it.

This method is not to be mistaken as threatening the customer or using fear sales. Selling through fear has many shortcomings and is not sustainable, because, post the initial purchase, the customer's logic overrides their moments of fear and buyer's remorse occurs, leading the customer to cancel, demand a refund and share negative feedback to friends. The suggested method here is used when the salesperson has identified that the customer is more eager to avoid losing than they are to gain savings. In the retail banking industry, salespeople can share with the customer, "The more days that you wait to move your funds into a savings/investment account, the more days it is costing you to keep it in your transaction account."

Not everyone is out to win—however, no one likes to accept that they are about to lose. Avoiding pain is a strong and enduring motivator for customers. Once the customer realises that it is more painful to live without the product than it is to purchase it, you have the sale. At the end of the day, the cost involved will eventually pay for the product. In the words of Zig Ziglar, "People buy what they want when they want it more than they want the money it costs."

HONESTY IS THE ONLY POLICY

In your recommendation to a customer, you will be displaying your product's most pronounced features and benefits to wow them. Of course, there is nothing wrong with this; however, sometimes when we hear a long series of good news, our sceptical minds wonder, "This has to be too good to be true." Our customers are not immune to this level of scepticism, which reflects in their question, "So what's the catch?"

Traditionally, salespeople put on the cheesiest smile and say, "There is no catch." Unfortunately, this response lacks the compelling facts and reasons that sceptic customers need in order to shift their perception. Instead, we should read one layer deeper into what the customer is actually saying when they ask that question. When a customer says, "What's the catch?" what they are actually say is, "It sounds great and I want to get it—I just don't want to get ripped off or later realise that you benefited from this transaction more than I did." So how do you satisfy a sceptic? By using the overcompensated truth. If there is a reason your organisation has advertised a very strong offer, then give the customer the respect they deserve and tell them. There is no harm in saying, "The only condition on this offer is for you to organise the delivery a week later" or, "As an organisation, we have invested in these types of offers to attract more new customers." Why would anyone have a problem with that? That type of direct honesty will quiet the loud cynical voice in their minds, making room for logic and reason. Remember; if the customer is asking questions like this, they want the product and are just waiting for you to sell it to them. To quote Zig Ziglar again, "Honesty is not the best policy; it's the only policy".

KEEP IT SIMPLE

In this day and age, if a customer has approached a salesperson rather than going online, they are seeking a human being to be able to explain their products and take the complexity out of the decision-making process. If the process was simple, they would it themselves. It is important that we adopt the following tips in keeping it simple:

AVOID EXCESSIVE DETAIL

Many salespeople have expressed that they feel guilty or unethical unless they have explained every single detail to the customer. Now, unless this is in relation to products and services that are heavily scrutinised by regulatory bodies such as pharmacy, banking or insurance, then the only outcome that you are guaranteeing is the customer's confusion. If you are selling furniture, there is no need to explain every detail of how the sofa has been designed and made unless this aligns with the values and interests of the customer. Once you have uncovered what is important to them to make a decision, focus on those things—everything else is superfluous excess detail. Those important elements are all that the customer wants to hear and they are the reasons for which they would buy. Of course, we should feel free to share terms and conditions with the customer where necessary; however, let's not overburden the decision-making process with undue information.

Overly descriptive product brochures can also be a distraction and we should be wary of this when using them. More often than not, people are confused by all of the options and they leave without deciding, in the fear of making the wrong choice. Having a list of product options can leave customers with the feeling of missed opportunity as all products have their own unique advantage. Kill the product brochure and trust in your ability to have a high-quality conversation.

Remember; the things that matter to you as an expert might not matter to the customer.

MAKE RECOMMENDATIONS SPECIFIC

The closer and more specifically that you can align your recommendation with the customer's needs, the more attractive your product will appear. This will also assist the customer in making a decision with more confidence. Any detail outside of the specific needs of the customer can clutter the decision and unnecessarily give the client more information to digest.

TALK ABOUT THE PRODUCT IN PRACTICAL TERMS

A common enemy of simplicity is speaking in theoretical abstract. Explaining product features without relating it to practical examples places too much pressure on the customer to think, which will cause doubt. If you were to sell a television, for example, and needed to explain the picture quality, you should avoid talking about the intricate details of the contrast ratio. (a measurement of the depth of colour that shows the difference between the brightest white colour and the darkest black on the television), for example. Very few customers will understand this and be able to translate it into a tangible benefit. If you wish to make it simple, provide a practical example such as, "You mentioned that your family watches movies—and the great thing about this television is that it contains more colours than most TVs. When you're watching that next movie, the picture will be brighter, clearer, richer and much closer to what the film director intended."

Asking open-ended questions earlier in the sales process will help you find the most appropriate examples to share.

AVOID BRAND/INDUSTRY TERMINOLOGY

In the process of demonstrating the features and benefits of your organisation's products, we need to remember that our customers have not participated in an induction training with your company, nor should we assume that they understand industry terminology and concepts. At times we need to slow down and explain ourselves without being impatient with the customer's lack of knowledge in our offering.

I witnessed a case of this error when I was consulting with a retail bank in Australia. The conversation was between a staff member and a customer who only held one transaction account with the bank. The staff member identified an opportunity to sell the customer a savings/investment account, which is a high-interest-bearing online account. The staff member looked at the customer and said, "I have identified an opportunity to make you money and save you fees through a savings account." Confused, the customer responds by saying, "Um, I have a savings account with you guys," to which the staff member responded, "No, you only have an Everyday Account." Even more confused, the customer says, "Yes, I use my savings account every day. I know this is a savings account because when I go to the ATM, I press savings."

This poor customer! How on earth was she supposed to know what an 'Everyday Account' was or to know the difference between a transaction account and savings account? To bank employees and financially savvy customers this is obvious— however, not for anyone else.

Instead, what the staff member should have said was, "I can see that you have a transaction account that you use for your day-to-day spending and access to cash. All of the funds that you have placed in there are not earning any interest for you. Instead, we can open an additional fee-free account that gives you online access to your funds and earns you 5% interest every year."

BUNDLING VS. INDIVIDUAL PRODUCTS

In multi-product sales environments where cross-selling is common practice, many salespeople have fallen into the trap of selling each additional item as its own individual product, rather than as part of a single package. This long-drawn-out conversation is overwhelming for the customer and it not only multiplies the decision-making process but it also multiplies the amount of questions, objections and decisions the customer will have to make.

Imagine that you were in the market to purchase a desktop computer. You meet with a salesperson and he explains all of the features of the computer, and you are satisfied with his explanations. Once you are happy to buy, he further explains that you will also need a monitor, and after finding the best monitor, he starts to talk about a mouse, then a keyboard and then a printer. This has made a difficult conversation impossible.

The solution to this is simple: always sell as a package. When you sell in a package, you can reduce the complexity of multiple sales into one conversation, which will consist of one series of questions and objections. For the customer, they now only need to make one decision and are getting the value that they deserve by coming in to see you, as opposed to using a self-service method like your company's website. Think about the products that you sell: do any of your products complement each other? Is there an opportunity to bundle them together into a package?

GIVE LESS OPTIONS

In the guise of good intentions, a sense of guilt, fear of manipulation and an unspoken moral obligation to humanity, we see countless examples of salespeople giving customers lots of options to choose from. When this approach has been challenged in sales seminars, a range of excuses have been shared such as, "At the end of the day, they should choose" or, "They are entitled to choose" or, "They know what they want" or, "I feel that it is unethical when I recommend one option," These feelings are flawed as they tend to achieve the opposite outcome to what is intended. If we are using the above quotes, we need to reassess what it is that we are there to do. A customer does not speak to a salesperson to have him read out the brochure and make the customer choose. They want to have things explained, questions answered, and for the process to be simple.

Trust in the process of selling and trust in yourself. If you have asked an ample amount of questions and know what the most appropriate choice is, don't confuse the customer with options— be bold and give them one recommendation. If you are in a situation where you do not know what the right recommendation is, then it is simple: you didn't ask enough questions. If you leave the customer, they will be thinking, 'I came to you to help me figure this out.' Our perception of what we think is right for the customer may not be what they actually *want*. Do not be afraid to deliver what the customer is expecting from you.

MANAGING EXPECTATIONS

We will often meet customers who want to cut through the process of questions and just want us to take them through the products or tell them which one is the best. Of course, adopting a value-add selling mindset, we know that the best product is the one that best meets the needs of the customer; however, the customer may still insist on not responding questions and just want a run-through of all of your options in order for them to make a decision. There are many ways out of this, of course, however you will certainly encounter dominant customers that will persist and force you down this path. Giving in to the customer's desires to view all of the options and skip questions is risky. Let's explore some commonly practised methods for comparing options.

Spinning up is a common sales practice as opposed to a widely taught methodology. This is where the salesperson starts the recommendation from the lowest-tier product and then moves their way up to the premium options. This is a poor management of expectations as customers see the standard product as an option and begin to imagine life with it. Even if it doesn't satisfy their needs, the customer still forces their mind to generate a picture of what life would be like with this option and a certain degree of acceptance will be agreed. This includes the features of the product and the price. The next option you show them may be more appealing as it is what they previously expected, plus more; however, now they are less likely to accept the price of the higher-tier product as they have mentally accepted the lower price. The customer can also perceive all of the extra features and unnecessary bells and whistles. This only confuses the customer ("I need to think about it") and results in objections ("That's too expensive").

Spinning down is occasionally practised and commonly taught. This is where the salesperson starts by showing the highest-tier option and working their way down. This is very common in selling new cars, where they will show the best car that they have and then you cut out features that you don't need. The intent here is to set the price expectations high and make everything else seem like a bargain.

What these car salespeople do not understand is that, just like with *spinning up*, customers imagine life with that product, and removing features from the equation is like snatching it out of their hand. Suddenly every option that you display seems comparatively unappealing and inferior to their perception of what they want.

To bring to life the flaw in these sales practices, imagine a Credit Card salesperson who knows that a customer needs to get a standard card with reward points, based on the questions asked. Then imagine that they show them the standard rewards card and also the Platinum option. Immediately your recommendation appears inferior. They will not buy the Platinum as its price may exceed expectations and they will not buy the standard as it now seems like a cheap version of the Platinum.

So if we can't spin up or down, what do we do? The ideal answer: trust in the process of asking questions in order for you to make the right recommendation. The next time a customer pressures you to start product-flogging and asks, "How much is the best one?" or, "Run me through your products," you can confidently liken your products to the services of a mechanic and say, "To tell you the best product for you without asking you questions is like a mechanic fixing your car without having a look to see what is wrong with it. In order for me to customise a package that will benefit you, I want to start by asking…."

Stand firm to the process that is most beneficial to the customer. They will appreciate it. Do not waiver from your high standards of customer-centric selling because a client applies pressure. You would prefer to justify your questions now, than have to wait 6 months to explain to the customer why you sold them a product that they did not need.

But What if They Really Persist?

The above was the ideal approach, however we have all met customers that demand a comparison to your other products. Of course we do not want to hide anything from the customer or be manipulative. We are trying to create a superior experience for the customer. So, what do we do when the customer persists?

In this case show an option that does the opposite of meeting their needs, like a credit card with no reward points and the bells and whistles that they want. Suddenly the correct option becomes easier to decide upon and the customer feels confident with their decision-making. Customers ask for comparisons in the fear of missing out on something unknown. Give them the confidence that you can recommend the right option for them.

7 OVERCOMING OBJECTIONS

For most people working in sales, objections are the part of the process that they fear the most. They feel that objections are confrontational, negative, aggressive, counterproductive, and sometimes it is hard not to take it personally. This is how they appear on the surface—but fortunately, when we dig deep, these feelings are mostly myths and only represent one perception of objections. Objections are a natural part of the buying process—whether you like it or not, they are here to stay. We need to become more familiar with them if we want to survive in sales. We need to learn how to welcome them and respond effectively.

OBJECTIONS—ARE THEY IMPORTANT?

As mentioned above, objections are a natural part of the buying process and not a failure of it. We need to accept them as a reality of sales. In fact, to go one step further, our very role as salespeople relies on the existence of objections. In this technological age where buying almost anything can be done online, why would someone approach you? What can you do that the Internet struggles with? The answer: having a conversation and responding to hard questions. Salespeople are in the business of handling objections—that is our unique function. It is why we will remain in business for a very long time. Therefore, to see the objections as an unfavourable part of sales process can be viewed as being ungrateful to the reason we have a job. Knowing that we shouldn't view objections as the unwanted pest of the conversation, then how should we see them?

We should welcome objections, as they can provide us feedback about our sales conversation and they make us better salespeople. If you are consistently receiving the same objection in every sales conversation, then there is clearly an area in which you are not positioning enough value. It is common that when a salesperson hears the same objection a number of times, they fear it and, rather than learning how to tackle it, they believe the objection to be true and therefore avoid the topic surrounding that objection. If someone is selling home furniture, for example, and customers regularly object to the time it takes to make and deliver, then that salesperson is likely to avoid bringing up the delivery time at all costs. The longer that we hide from that objection, the harder it will be to address it. Instead, we should see this is an opportunity to strengthen the sales presentation and become better salespeople.

Also, the higher you climb within your organisation, the more complex the sales conversation you are having, which leads to more difficult objections—therefore, we need to get good at them now, before it's too late.

WHOSE FAULT IS IT?

When receiving objections, it is very easy to blame the customer and think it is their fault, because they are stupid or annoying. At times, let's be honest, it could be true; however, the mindset of blaming the customer is not only illogical, but also counterproductive. If we believe it is the customer's fault, then there is no purpose in exerting effort in developing your skills in objection handling, as the outcome is predetermined. It is simply admitting that we as the salesperson have no influence over the buying process and the outcome was already decided by the customer before they met you.

Handling objections is the craft of the salesperson. We are in control. Athletes do not blame the weather for not getting a gold medal—dealing with challenges is what they do. Remember, the we all need salespeople to help us see value in that which will benefit us.

A PASSIONATE EXPRESSION OF VALUES

When a customer expresses an objection, they are usually not making irrelevant complaints. Our customers have better things to do than to invest time in telling us why they don't like our product. Therefore objections are less about why they don't like your product and more about what is most important to them when buying. When a customer says, "This is too expensive," what they are telling you is; price and/or value for money is important to them. Alternatively, if the customer says, "I'm too busy," they are telling you that time is important. Think about it; if it wasn't important, then why are they passionately expressing it? An objection is therefore just a passionate expression of values. This mind-shift can positively influence the way we think about objections and how we respond to them.

In the discovery part of the sales process, any salesperson would be celebrating if the customer revealed their values to them. Most customers are not even consciously aware that they have core buying values, which is why they are often expressed as an objection. In other words, an objection is a customer teaching you how to sell to them. By giving you the most important component of their decision-making process, they are saying, "If you want to get this sale, focus on my values."

When we hear objections, we should filter out the negative and focus in on the values that they are expressing, capitalise on it and match it with the corresponding benefits. If the objection was around convenience, keep coming back to the simple and easy features of your products. If the objection is around service, frequently mention the quality and efficiency of the service that the customer will receive. The reasons for which you assume the customer will not buy are often the reasons they will.

WHAT DO WE CALL OBJECTIONS?

In sales training, we label these expressions of values as 'objections;' however, this is not the best way to label it when speaking to the customer, as they might not see it this way. Acknowledging that it is an objection makes the customer feel annoying, hard to deal with or as if they are bothering you. We should never refer to an objection as an objection. You will find it harder to defuse, which will unnecessarily create a barrier between the customer and a buying outcome.

Instead, we could refer to them as "an important question" or "an insightful point". Remember, we want to hear any objections that they have, so we know what they value and what could potentially be holding them back. So when you are responding to an objection, we could say, "You've raised an interesting point. Thank you for asking that; it's a really important question."

Maintaining rapport must continue throughout the whole sales process and we want to keep making the customer feel important and acknowledged.

TIME-WASTERS

In my experience, I have heard a lot of salespeople refer to objecting customers who have objections as *time-wasters*. Remember, if they are expressing their values, this is the opposite of *time-wasting*. How ecstatic would you be if every customer taught you how to sell to them and expressed the elements of your product to focus on to get them to buy? This is far from a time-waster—this is your ideal customer.

THE REASONS WHY PEOPLE OBJECT

In order to get better at responding to objections, preparation is needed. We need to start thinking about the all of the different types of objections that we may get and build some generic proof points against these objection types. Now, I am not saying that we necessarily need to build a fully fledged script or a one-size-fits-all approach to objection handling; rather, we need to know why those objections are not true and be confident in our response. If we fail to do this, we will always struggle to help the customer overcome this and get the products and services that can benefit them—and worst of all, we may hear the objection so many times that we end up believing it ourselves.

Zig Ziglar shared that there are five primary reasons why a customer will object. These are: no need, no money, no hurry, no desire and no trust. Let's explore these individually:

NO NEED

If the customer genuinely has no need for the product or service, it raises a number of questions. Have you qualified the customer up front? Is this product suitable to the customer? Have you explored how the customer will use the product? Have you played a numbers game and sold the product to just any customer? Are you using a generic script rather than tailoring your conversation to the customer's needs? Is it a conversation or just a presentation? Have you asked enough questions or did you do most of the talking? Has the customer misunderstood the product or how they will benefit? Did you share all of the proof points as to why this would add value to the customer?

NO MONEY

We should firstly acknowledge that there is definitely a group of customers who genuinely cannot afford to purchase your product; however, it is unlikely that these people will approach your company—or, alternatively, these customers would be identified when you ask qualifying questions. On the other hand, the majority of circumstances in which this objection is given are where the customer has not seen value in your product.

To put it simply, the money sitting in their bank account is more valuable to them than the perceived benefits of your product. This objection is a reflection on the quality of the sales conversation—have you demonstrated the value that the product brings? Have you linked the benefits of your product to the needs of the customer? What pleasure will the customer gain from buying your product? What pain can they avoid by buying? Are there enough objective reasons why your product is priced at that level? What value does the customer gain from the investment of their money?

No Hurry

This is a very common objection and an easy way out for the customer. The salesperson may have been able to effectively communicate the value of the product to the customer but have failed to answer the question, "Why should I buy it now and not later?"

What is the consequence if the customer does not buy now? This can be a very simple question to answer when we are selling medicine or crucial parts for a car; however, what if our product is not vital to them? Answering this question is very important in order to create a sense of urgency. I have witnessed countless times where a sales manager will push their sales force to create urgency around offers and limited-time promotions. I had an outbound salesperson call from a telecommunications provider telling me, "If you don't sign up now, you will miss out on the deal" and I have also heard a door-to-door salesperson tell me, "We are only in the area tonight; this your last chance." This type of urgency does more damage than good. First of all, we do not know how that individual likes to buy—perhaps they enjoy researching and asking friends, or having a long conversation with you, going through the terms and conditions. Rushing people without adding value about the long-term benefits of the product can lead to hasty decision-making and ultimately regret, cancellations and refunds.

Unjustified urgency can also have negative impacts on your overall brand. If you overemphasise the cut-off dates for your marketing campaign, it tells the customer that you won't wait for them or that you have approached them too late. If your urgency is similar to, "My manager said that I can only honour this offer if you sign up today," then you are telling the customer that, "My company has no patience for its customers nor do we have confidence that our product is valuable on its own." This is not to say that gifts with purchase are not important; however, the overemphasis on it can be detrimental to the sale. The desperation that a salesperson shows reflects the state of the organisation.

Despite the fact that these tactics may have been extremely successful between the '50s and the '80s, we need to remember that our customers have changed and are more educated on the sales process. In the market today, the power has shifted away from the organisation to the customer. Consumers know that if they call your company, write on your Facebook page and escalate the issue, then they will get whatever deal or offer you are claiming is no longer possible.

So if that is not how we go about creating urgency in this day and age, then how do we do it? Rather than making the urgency around the organisation's inflexibility or around the end date of a campaign, make it around the customer themselves. Display the opportunity gained and lost in order for the customer to build their own sense of urgency to get the product. In practical terms, you need to break down the benefit gained or lost each day that they delay the decision; for example, if you work in banking, there is generally a monetary urgency that you can create: "For every day that you delay not transferring your funds into our term deposit, you are missing out on $25. If you decide not to go ahead with it at all, it will be costing you $9,125 every year." In selling clothes, you can highlight the opportunities missed to wear the outfit. If you are selling tools, you can mention the amount of time waiting to repair an item or the chances of something else needing to be fixed.

Customer-based urgency empowers the customer by giving them the ownership of the decision. It does not discredit your brand or unnecessarily rush the customer—instead, it gives the customer logical reasons to make a more informed choice.

No Desire

Here are a few questions that you may wish to consider in order to diagnose the reasons for this objection. Are these customers even in the market to buy your product or service? Have you invested in enough questions to qualify the customer? Have you clearly matched the benefits of the product to the needs of the customer? What is their need? Do your products fulfil that need? Have you uncovered what is important to them? What do they desire?

No Trust

There are three things that the customer needs to trust in order to make an informed buying decision—that is, trust in you, trust in your organisation and trust in your product. If the customer does not trust any of these things, they will not buy.

Let's revisit some of the content shared in previous chapters on trust that relate to this objection type. If the customer does not trust you, have you demonstrated that you are worthy of their trust? Have you been open and honest about the product? Have you showed integrity by over-sharing detail in an attempt to show all of your cards? Have you revealed all of the hidden costs? Was your explanation detailed to ensure the customer has a clear understanding? Is your body language congruent with your message? Are you giving the customer eye contact or are your eyes nervously wandering around? Do you see yourself as an expert before expecting the customer to see you as one?

This last point, about seeing yourself as an expert, is heavily underplayed for people who are new to sales. Think about how an expert, like a doctor, builder or financial planner speaks. They are confident in sharing what is right for their client and can add insights about their product that the customer could not have found on their own. These professionals recognise that their clients need them and they spend their time adding value. If you have undergone training, know your product, and are qualified to represent an organisation in sales, guess what? You are an expert! Speak with the confidence that you have earned and don't be afraid of knowing more than the customer, as that is what they came to you for.

In order for people to trust you, do you have a strong personal brand? How do you introduce yourself to the customer? Do you articulate who are you, what you do, and how you can benefit the customer? You may be thinking, "Well, the customer doesn't care about who I am." True. They don't want your life story; however, they do want reassurance that you are the best person to speak to on their topic of concern. Many times a customer will not buy simply because they don't know you or they are more comfortable dealing with someone they have spoken to previously. Accelerate the process of rapport by giving the customer a reason to like and trust you.

When introducing yourself, when opening a series of questions or making recommendations, don't be shy to state your values as a salesperson. This will give your customer reasons to trust you. With great confidence, you should tell the customer that you pride yourself in delivering exceptional outcomes for your clients. If the customer feels overwhelmed by this level of energy, you can use a line that Jordan Belfort (formerly known as *the Wolf of Wall Street*) uses in his course, *Straight Line Persuasion*, which is, "Please don't misconstrue my enthusiasm for pressure."

A mistake that many salespeople make is forgetting to talk about the power of their organisation and what they stand for, telling the customer that, "This company prides itself in its ability to satisfy our customers," or, "Last year Company ABC won the award for...". Even if you believe that your competitors produce the same value, it does not mean that we should not mention this. The customer may not be thinking about your competitors, but rather only analysing whether they want to invest their hard-earned money in your organisation. Also, your competitors are most likely not speaking about the strength of their brand—and this can be your edge. Sell the benefits that your company offers for free and shout them from the roof top. These are usually the services and company values that employees take for granted—however, they can be a wow factor for our customers.

If the customer is doubtful about the product and does not trust that it will deliver a benefit that meets their need, then demonstrate your product, share customer testimonials, tell them how the goods are designed and built, share personal experiences with the product or give them the statistics around how many people buy that product every year.

Reading through these objection types and addressing the questions and comments within each one will hopefully demonstrate that customers do not own the objections process— we do!

SEEKING OUT OBJECTIONS

It is now clear that there is no need to avoid objections altogether, as they are a critical part of the sales process. To take it one step further, we should also seek them out in order to address the most important aspects of the buying decision for the customer. Objections do not only exist in speech and many are left unexpressed, lingering in the customer's mind. This can be challenging for the salesperson as they may be steering the conversation blindfolded. This is not to say that if the customer does not have any objections internally stored or expressed then we are doomed—instead, we wish to ensure that all of our bases are covered.

If you can see unease with the customer through their body language, facial expressions, things they say or hesitancy to answer questions, you may wish to invite them to express their concern/question: "I can see that you are interested in our product; however, there seem to be areas that I have not addressed. May I ask what they are?" Being proactive with the customer's objections is both professional and courteous. It will also enhance levels of rapport and trust with the customer. Without doing this, you end up in a stalemate and cannot advance the sales process.

In some conversations and scenarios, it is appropriate to bring out the objection at the beginning of the conversation; for example, if the customer has been shopping around among all of your competitors and not bought anything, you may wish to ask the reasons why. Remember; drawing out these objections is a key way for you to uncover their values. This also arms you with the most effective areas to address throughout the conversation.

READING THE SUBTITLES

While we know that objections are the customer expressing their values, we should recognise that they may not be articulating their point in its totality. Often, an objection has an underlying message behind it that we need to uncover. A close friend of mine and entrepreneur, Steve Roberts, always used to say that when he was at a sales call, he would dig deeper into what the customer is actually saying by "reading the subtitles".

Whenever a customer gave an objection, he would literally imagine subtitles written below them translating what they have said into something useful and something that he can act upon. When a customer said to him "It's too expensive," for example, he would read the subtitles as, "If you could show me a way that the benefits outweigh the price, then I am ready to buy." If the customer objects with, "I don't have time to talk about this," it could mean, "If you give me a compelling reason to invest time with you, I will stay." When a client says, "I need to ask my partner," often what they are saying is, "The last thing I want to do is take this product home and have an argument with my partner over my mistake," or, "Please give me some compelling dot points to use when selling the idea to my partner."

Of course these subtitles are not accurate, are highly assumptive and will be contradicted in the following section about clarifying objections; however, recognising that there is more to an objection than what is on the surface is an important mindset that we can choose to adopt. When Steve understood the objection in this light, his responses and questions were a lot more optimistic and less confrontational. He was giving the customer the best chance to make the right decision and never gave up in the face of an objection. He did not assume that this was the customer's opinion—which we will explore next. Instead, he just chose the most positive outlook in order to shape his own behaviours.

THE DANGER OF ASSUMING

We are always told to never assume—and people like to use the first three letters of the word *assume* to describe us when we do. So why is it so bad? If I am an experienced salesperson and day in and day out I hear the same objections every single time, surely I know what it means, right? If you are an experienced salesperson, you will know that this is far from true.

Beware of making the mistake of assuming that you understand the history, the context, the reasons, the beliefs, the values and the nature of the objection before clarifying first. So often I see the overly confident salesperson's knee-jerk reaction to answer the objection without exploring the underlying message. When I worked for a subscription television company, customers would regularly say, "That's too expensive" and then the salesperson would excitedly jump up and demonstrate how the monthly subscription was great value and all of these features and benefits that you can't get anywhere else! They would go on to explain how the subscription fee is the equivalent of a coffee a day and how it is cheaper than renting movies every day. Then there would be an awkward pause and the customer would say, "I was talking about the installation cost."

Now look what you have done! You have shown the customer that you do not care enough to explore what is important to them, and instead you have rambled on about your product. You have shown them that you care more about the sale than their satisfaction—and, worst of all, now you have the customer doubtful about the monthly subscription, which they may not have been worried about before! You have become like a doctor who prescribes medication without attempting a diagnosis.

Individuals who are making the shift from service to sales usually intend on having the customer at the centre, and it is critical that we accompany this mindset with the right techniques to show the customer how important they are. When a customer gives you an objection that could have more than one meaning, ensure that you ask them to expand, clarify or explore further so that you can effectively respond while demonstrating to the customer that you care. Remember, if an objection is an expression of values where the customer is boldly voicing what is important to them, it is definitely worth investing your time to dig deeper on the topic and not to dismiss it.

Now, there is one simple rule for clarifying an objection, which is; *it is the salesperson who is aiming to learn more, rather than the customer being unclear.* If we respond to objections, for example, by saying, "I don't understand", "Please explain what you meant", "What do you mean?" we are telling the customer that they are a poor communicator. Remember, as you read their subtitles, they read yours too. Your question must come from a genuine sense of curiosity where you are seeking clarity in order to help them solve a problem. Response examples could be, "When you say it's too expensive, can you please expand on that?" or, "In order for me to find ways of adding value, can you please share more?"

This type of questioning empowers the customer to feel open about their objection rather than being embarrassed about it. They see that you are interested to learn more, which earns you more time with the customer.

Most objections have many possible meanings, so don't fall into the trap of thinking the ones you receive are one-sided. Below are some examples of what common objections can mean—of course, through clarifying, you will find many more:

OBJECTION	POTENTIAL MEANING
Too expensive	• I don't understand how this will benefit me
	• I am experiencing financial difficulty
	• Your competitor is cheaper
	• There is a particular fee that I was not expecting
	• The pricing structure seems too complex
	• My partner does not want me spending that much money
I don't have time	• I am in a rush to go somewhere else
	• This conversation is boring
	• I am not in the market to buy this
	• I don't understand your products
	• I will not have time to use your product
	• The application process seems long, but I could come back later
	• Is there any easier way to do this?
I am not interested	• I don't understand what you are selling
	• I already have this product
	• I don't like salespeople
	• I am not sure how this will benefit me
	• This seems expensive

OBJECTION	POTENTIAL MEANING
I need to think about it	• I am confused
	• You spoke too fast
	• I need to consult with my partner
	• I am not the decision-maker
	• I am going to investigate your competitors
	• I need to assess my financial position

YOU JUST DON'T UNDERSTAND

After four seasons of experience selling any product, you should have a clear idea of the most common objections and typical customer scenarios. With knowledge, skill and practice, this will give you confidence in responding to them; however, we should not mistake this confidence for a deep understanding of each and every customer situation.

On countless occasions, I have witnessed salespeople respond to objections with "I understand" or, worse, "I understand how you feel." So what is so wrong with this approach? Imagine if the customer says, "I can't afford it," and you respond with "I understand how you feel" and genuinely you do as this product may be out of your price range as well. Is that what the customer is thinking? Not necessarily. Instead, they will be running a frustrated internal dialogue in their minds, asking, "How could you understand how I feel? You haven't lost your job—you're working," or, "Did your partner leave you and take half of your money?" If the objection was, "I don't have time" and you responded with, "I understand how you feel," they may be thinking, "I'm late to pick up my children—how could you understand how I feel? You're being paid to be here and have nowhere to go." The examples are limitless.

Just because you have experienced a financial hardship or a lack of time does not mean that you understand how the customer feels. Customers are very savvy and sensitive to our language, and saying that you understand a situation the customer has expressed to you can be seen as trivialising it or undermining its value. Remember; objections are expressions of the customer's values.

The unfortunate thing is that this wording is taught in many sales methodologies through the technique of *'feel, felt, found'*. Sales trainers and authors sell it like it's the latest and greatest thing; however truth be told, it is one of the oldest methods of objection handling and it has been around longer than you have. This can only mean one thing—our customers have heard this over and over again. Each time they have expressed their values in the form of an objection, they would have heard someone respond with, "I understand how you feel." It has lost its power, and its meaning has changed. The market and the understanding of customers have evolved—so let's evolve the way we speak.

As a salesperson, you often do not know your customers on an intimate level, so rather than *'understanding'*, all we have done is heard their concern. You can easily replace the phrase, 'I understand how you feel' by saying:

- I can see that your time is important to you

- I recognise that you want to get value out of your purchase

- I respect that you don't want to make a purchase out of your budget

- I acknowledge that you perceive the price to be high

By using this language, we are not agreeing with the customer, nor are we pretending that we understand. We are simply acknowledging what the customer has expressed, and demonstrating that we are willing to listen. By doing this, we have maintained rapport and the customer will know that we have some more to share with them.

To take it even one step further, sometimes we can openly acknowledge that we do not understand; for example, if the customer says "I have been cheated by a salesperson before," you can say, "I am genuinely sorry to hear that and I can't even imagine what it would have been like to have your trust abused like that."

Remember, as an expert, you possess knowledge on your subject, and as a professional you make observations—however, unless you are psychologist you should never claim to understand people's emotions.

Agreeing Without Agreeing

When a customer delivers an objection, they believe they are correct, much like when two people argue and somehow they both feel that they are right. In some cases the customer is expecting a battle where both parties are trying to prove the other wrong, and it gives them further opportunities to strengthen their resolve in their original argument. So how can you defuse this? Well at some stage, you need to find some point of agreement. You may not of course agree with their entire objection, but you must search for mutual ground.

In Dale Carnegie's famous book *How to Win Friends and Influence People,* he shares how, when the point of agreement is found, the argument stops. So how do we agree when we disagree? A classic example is when the customer's objection is around the integrity of your organisation—they might say, "Your company is full of cheats." Now, agreeing with them does not mean that we say, "Mr Customer, you are spot on! You have never seen a business with more cheats than ours!" Instead, you may like to say, "Knowing that you are a long-standing customer, I am positive that you have an excellent reason for saying this. Can you please expand on it?" In this scenario, we are not agreeing that our organisation is full of cheats; instead, we are agreeing that the customer would have a good reason to make such a comment.

The customer could also say, "Your products are poor quality" and we will find mutual ground by saying, "I recognise that it is important to find products that are of high quality before making a purchasing decision" and then you continue to explain how your product meets that high standard. Finding good-quality products would become a common point of agreement between you and the customer. Finding mutual agreement helps you maintain rapport and defuse any unnecessary tension between you and the customer.

WHAT IF THE OBJECTION IS WRONG?

There will be many circumstances where the customer's objection is categorically incorrect or is based on a false/limited understanding. Your products may have widely accepted myths circulating around and are brought up regularly by customers. For example, there could be a rumour about your organisations privacy policy and the lack of security of the customer's personal details. As we are all very passionate about the products and services that we sell, it is easy to fall into the trap of getting defensive and to unintentionally sound as if we care about the company more than the customer.

Instead, we should take this opportunity to educate the customer without making them feel stupid. We could respond by simply saying, "I am glad that you asked about our privacy policy; you reminded me that I have not shared one of the great security features of our products."

FILTERING EXCUSES FROM REAL OBJECTIONS

Depending on the nature of the objection, at times you may become unsure whether it is a genuine objection or just an excuse. If it is an excuse, the prospect may not even be listening to your responses and move from one objection to another trying to wriggle out of the conversation. This makes the continuity of the conversation very challenging as it will lack of logical flow. On the other hand, if the objection is genuine, you are able to have a coherent conversation and the customer will be attentively listening.

To test whether an objection is an excuse or genuine, we need to ask effective questions. If the objection was on price, for example, after clarifying you can filter the excuses out by asking, "If I could show a solution within your price range, would that be worth speaking about?" or, "If, hypothetically, the value of our products outweighed the cost, would that be something worth talking about?" If the objection is genuine, then the answer is yes and the conversation continues; if it is merely an excuse, then they will irrationally stand by their objection.

'I NEED TO THINK ABOUT IT'

One of the most common ways that an unsuccessful sales conversation ends is, "I need to think about it" or, "Can I take away a brochure?" or, "Let me do some further research and I will get back to you." So let's read the subtitles on this and uncover what this really means so that we can adopt the most useful mindset. If towards the end of the conversation the customer says that they "need to think about it", it is typically an excuse or a euphemism for, "You have overwhelmed me with too many options" or, "I don't understand what you are saying." These objections traditionally happen in scenarios where the salesperson did most of the talking. How do I know this? Had the customer spoken earlier, the salesperson would have identified that they were confused or they needed additional time to digest the information.

This is a great objection as it is just another way that the customer is giving you feedback, meaning you still have a chance to recover the sale. There are a number of ways to respond to this—and please choose an option that suits your product, company and, most important, your customer:

UNCOVER THE CONFUSION

"I appreciate that you need time to make the right decision. Can I ask, are there any areas that I could clarify now, which would make your decision easier?"

TAKE RESPONSIBILITY

"I recognise that I may have been unclear in parts of the conversation; which area can I cover again in order for you to make the right decision?"

INCREASING URGENCY

"It is important that you have the time to think about this decision and I want to help accelerate this process so you can receive these benefits faster. Please take your time while I am here so I can answer any questions."

NEED FOR AN EXPERT

"Fantastic. The best time and place to think about it is here, where you have all of the information and a subject matter expert available to answer any questions that arise." Or

"Great. Let's think about it together, because if you go home and think about it alone, I will not be there to answer any questions that are not in the brochure or on our website."

At an initial glance, using any of these approaches may feel pushy; however, let's take a look from the customer's perspective. The customer is feeling that they are not armed with enough compelling facts to make a decision. Remember, you are a paid expert who is hired to help them. If you fail to persist, you have done the customer a disservice.

'TOO EXPENSIVE'

Unless we are selling free energy-saving light bulbs door-to-door, we have all heard the price objection before. Most salespeople hear this objection often enough to justify adding it to their job descriptions. Assuming that you have qualified the customer and know that this product is within their realm of affordability (i.e., you are you are not selling an S-Class Mercedes to someone with a $10,000 budget) the price objection is often a knee-jerk reaction rather than a genuine objection. There are countless examples of the one customer finding a small item in one store too expensive and then happily buying an expensive bag, wearing a designer suit, or asking for that extra luxury feature when buying a car. Remember, there is a distinct difference between being able to afford something and one's willingness to buy, so let's be conscious not to mix up affordability and one's perception of value.

Dig deeper with these customers because often they are not saying, "I do not have enough money in my bank account to be able to afford your product"—if this was the case, why would they be there? Instead, their subtitles are often reading, "The money that I have earned which is sitting in the bank is worth more than the value that you have demonstrated in your product." So does this mean we need to lower the price? The answer is no, despite what most companies do. An exotic loose-leaf tea manufacturer that I consulted with was lacking in sales for their initial launch, and their first reaction was to lower their price, despite the fact that they are already cheaper than their next closest competitor. Will this really make a difference? Can people really not afford $14 for a few months' worth of tea? One start-up company who sell decorative artwork and wall-art for children could not get sales off the ground and immediately wanted to lower their price. Customers who are into decorating are spending beyond their basic needs, and traditionally have more than $50 in their account.

So if I advised both the tea maker and the artist not to lower their price, what advice did I give them? Raise your value! If the ratio between price and value is imbalanced in favour of protecting one's money, then raise your value to make the purchase an investment rather than a cost. Lowering your price can have detrimental effects to both the appeal/perception of your product and, importantly, your bottom line. As a customer, if you already don't want a product because you do not see value in it, a cheaper version of it will not make it more appealing. Instead, it will only remind you why the product or service is not valuable in the first place.

We must clarify to learn exactly why the price outweighs the value. When clarifying the objection, uncover what is important to the customer—ensuring that you have explained and demonstrated the corresponding benefits of your product. Remember; value is a perception and perceptions are based on life experiences. Therefore, the areas that you and your organisation find important may not relate to the desires of the customer.

Gaining leverage and shifting the power of negotiation is another motivator for expressing this objection. Customers believe that they can shift the price by haggling, and even if they can't, it is worth giving it a try. This is born from inconsistencies in shopping experiences in different industries. Most large businesses have empowered their sales force or frontline management with a range to move on price within their profit margin, and therefore customers impose this rule upon you and your business. This leverage can only work when the salesperson does not have belief and conviction in their product or service, or understand the value that their product delivers.

Now that we have extensively explored the context behind this objection, let's see how we can respond to it:

VALUE VS. PRICE

This is a very preventable objection, for two reasons: First, you should invest your time in the conversation, to customise the product's value proposition to the customer's needs to a point that it makes the price look insignificant. And the second reason is that the customer should not even know the price until you are confident that they see value in your offering.

In the book *Secrets of Closing the Sales,* Ziglar draws a distinction between price and cost—price being how much money it requires to purchase a product, and cost being how much you save or lose by making the decision to buy. Ziglar encourages us to say, "Some companies beat us on price, but we win on cost"—that is, in the long run, it will you cost you more to replace and repair the cheaper ones in the market. When justifying the price Ziglar suggests that we say, "A few years ago, our organisation made a decision that it would be easier to explain price once than to constantly apologise for quality."

If you have caught yourself in this scenario, you may wish to say, "Unlike many of our competitors, our products provide a long-term benefit. While your traditional [insert product type] that costs $100 will last eight months until you need to replace it for another $100 one, our customers are continuing to see benefits from ours for over two years at the price of $150. When you calculate the value of these products, our competitors' products can cost you $300 over two years, where ours is only $150."

If you don't know what the long-term value benefit of your product is, you should calculate it. For services that are based on subscriptions, it may not be as easy to calculate; instead, you will need to do the opposite and calculate the daily benefits of the product. Instead of saying "$30 a month", it could be "a dollar a day".

The other angle could be raising value by comparison. A friend of mine is starting up her own photography business with a very fair price point. She used to get stumped on this objection on a regular basis, until she was able to break down the product offering and also compare it with the customer going elsewhere.

"Our service entails more than just a series of photos. We have a comprehensive consultation to learn more about you and your family before we do the shoot. We then select a set location to suit the tone of the photo shoot. I will then spend three hours with you to complete the photos, and when I take them away, I will assess each photo and recommend a number of them for the final album. I then edit the photos that you have selected and customise them to suit your album design. Then we book in a consultation to ensure that it has met your expectations, before I produce the photos. Each of these is significantly costly and will entail 50 hours of labour. This is why we are so proud of our fair price of $1500."

BARGAINING

As mentioned, due to inconsistencies in how merchants price their products and manage discounts, consumers feel the right to bargain at any store. If your business does not have this contingency available, then it places a lot of pressure on salespeople.

You should take pride in your prices and explain their reason. Some customers think that if a product costs $20 to make, then it should be sold for $21 dollars. Explaining what the price does for the customer and the organisation will rationalise the figure and empower the salesperson to stand by their price. Here is an example of this:

"We take great pride in our pricing as it is fairly based on a balance between the costs involved to produce such high-quality goods and the investments required to continue to innovate for our customers and enhance the quality of our service. Moving on this figure would mean decreasing long-term innovation and investment back to you, which is something that we are not willing to do."

Be confident about the quality of your product—and the price becomes insignificant!

'JUST LOOKING'

If you are working in a retail store, you would have heard many customers saying, "Just looking". Since it is heard so often, rather than learning how to tackle it, I have observed that most salespeople accept it as a reality. This acceptance dampens confidence and by the middle of the day after you have heard, "Just looking" so many times, it is easy to give up on proactively approaching customers.

There are two types of customers who are 'just looking': those who resist being sold to, and those who are genuinely browsing or window-shopping. Either way, it will be hard to figure out which one they are by not speaking to them, so let's explore how to overcome this.

Let's try and see it from the lens of a customer. This is not hard, as we are all customers of other stores and we have all done this before. So what would it take for you to go from 'just looking' to wanting to speak with the salesperson? What would they have to say? What could they do to make you feel comfortable and remove all of the pressure of unwanted impulse buying? We know that the same old script of telling you what items are on sale is far too generic and that it hardly interests the genuine shoppers—so what does?

To avoid assuming which type of 'just looking' your customer is, you will need to say something that gives you room to answer that question. Remember, in order to get a desired behaviour from the customer, we need to give them something first—the law of reciprocity!

First of all, approach the customer with a smile—they are contagious; you are bound to receive one in return—and introduce yourself. I seriously cannot remember the last time I went to purchase clothes, electronics or furniture where the salesperson gave me their name. Relieve them of the pressure of being haunted by a salesperson by encouraging them to take their time and allowing them to look/use/try as long as they want. Lastly, give a warm invitation to speak to you when they are ready. By 'warm' I don't mean "See me when you're ready". Instead, you should make them feel comfortable by saying, "I would be delighted to help you find the right option, so when you have questions or if you have not found what you are looking for, please come and see me.".

This will not get every single customer to dive at your feet begging for your service; however, it will give you the best fighting chance to lead to a conversation.

'I'VE BEEN BURNT IN THE PAST'

Negative experiences with your organisation or a competitor can easily be carried over with the customer. When a customer shows resistance and distrust telling you that they "have been burnt in the past" allow the customer to express themselves, as getting 'burnt' may be related to service, salespeople, company policy, product failures or unpleasant features. Reassuring the customer that it will never happen to them again, is not enough, as we can be confident that they have been told that before. In order to shift this perception of your brand or product, the proof of such bold statements will need to be demonstrated.

This type of objection also provides a great opportunity to wow the customer, which may be easier than you think as their expectations will be low. Remember, customers discover value through relativity and comparison. Focus your conversation on the offerings of your company that are at variance with their poor experience. The customer will be observing carefully through a thick lens of scepticism; however, when they see signs of the opposite to their expectation, they will be reassured that this objection is no longer relevant.

Respond to this objection through deeds, not words alone.

'I AM SCARED THAT I WILL REGRET THIS'

In a plenary presentation at a conference in Australia, my best friend and part-time genius, Faya Hayati, who is an economist at the World Bank once spoke about the power of regret saying, "The scent of regret inhaled but once will remain with you forever." I always told him that I would put that in a book one day and, as best friends do, he laughed in my face. As I hate to admit it—and he loves to hear it—this quote is spot-on. Regret is easily achieved and difficult to shake off. Customers fear regret as they despise loss of time, money and opportunities.

Before exploring how we respond to this, let's stop using the most common response, which does not work: "Don't worry, sir; we have a cooling-off period" or, "You can always refund it within 90 days". Using a 'cooling-off period' or flexible refund policy in direct response to this objection may relieve some pressure regarding the long-term effects of regretful decision-making, but it shows desperation and you have not answered the underlying question (subtitles) which the customer is asking: "Can you please give me confidence beyond the least shadow of a doubt that I will not regret this decision?"

Understanding the psychology behind this objection is crucial as responding is relatively easy. Firstly, as you always do, clarify to ensure that you understand which element or perspective of the product they regret, and use facts and demonstrations to prove the invalidity of the fear of regret. Be detailed in sharing facts, as any vague response may affirm the initial doubt that the customer has.

Two months ago, my wife and I test-drove a car that we had been researching together. In a natural fear of regret, I asked the car salesperson, "What are the most common problems or regrets your customers have with this car?" His response: "People often regret that they didn't choose the upgraded package," which gives you a panoramic glass roof, LED lights and whole bunch of bells and whistles. He cleverly read my subtitles and, with confidence (not defensiveness), told me that people do not regret the purchase; they just want more of it.

'DO YOU GET COMMISSION FROM THE SALE?'

In general, people have less trust for salespeople when they know that they will be incentivised for the sale. This is not exactly an objection; however, if handled poorly, it can move the customer away from buying. To overcome this tension, it is important to be honest and show your belief in the integrity of what you do. Be proud of what you do and feel open to explain to the customer: "Yes, I am compensated for every customer who I help to find the right product."

We also want to demonstrate to the customer that the amount of commission that we receive is not so high that it would cloud our judgement or allow us to manipulate the customer in order to get a sale. Depending on the amount of commission you receive you may wish to use any variation of the following; "The amount that my company reward me for helping you today isn't enough to take my wife/husband out for lunch, but I know that it will certainly benefit you like it has helped many of my other customers"

OFFENCE AND DEFENCE

We should see the sales conversation as a process that begins in a neutral state and each part of the conversation either moves you towards a buying behaviour or further away. It is the salespersons role to maintain the conversation in the *positive* and it is every customer's right to delve into the *sceptical* to ensure they are making the correct decision.

For simplicity sake, let's say that an agreed benefit is in the positive and an objection brings the conversation into the sceptical. When you handle an objection you do not necessarily bring it back to the positive. More often than not, you are taking the conversation back to zero (neutral zone) as the taste of the customer's objection may still linger. So often I see salespeople do a magical performance in responding to an objection and move on once they feel that the customer is satisfied with the response.

Doing this is like playing a game of football where all of your players are in the defence standing in front of the goal box. It is true that you will very rarely lose a game with this approach and it is also true that it is equally difficult to win. The very best you can hope for is a tie. When we respond to an objection, we are in the defence and we have stopped a goal from being conceded. We then need to pass the ball up the field and remind our customers of the benefits in which met their needs and they were in agreement with—taking the conversation to the positive.

This is a critical step in the objection handling process and one that is often missed. Remember; never move on from the objection until the customer is left thinking about the benefits of the product and not the memory of their objection.

8 CLOSING THE SALE

Congratulations on making it this far. By now you will have read enough to guarantee an unshakable mindset about selling with integrity; you have established and maintained rapport with the customer; you have learnt a great deal about what the customer wants; you have engaged them in a meaningful and beneficial conversation about how you can meet their needs. The customer has expressed their values through a series of objections, to which you have responded in a logical and compelling way... So now what? It's time to deliver what the customer came in for. Close the sale.

MINDSET ON CLOSING THE SALE

Many people in sales don't enjoy closing the sale, for a variety of reasons: they feel pushy, fear rejection, afraid of losing rapport with the customer, or they are unsure if the customer is ready to buy. Before we explore why we should close the sale, let's take a deep dive into the cost of not closing the sale.

If you don't ask for the business, you have wasted the customer's time. You have talked to them for ten minutes to an hour about a product that you have not even given them an opportunity to buy. You have left the customer with a series of information which will assist them when they visit your competitors who are likely to close the sale. Of course, this is not the most important part of the sales process; however, its absence can make the preceding chapters fruitless.

Remember; if your customers have invested time to speak to you, undertaken the entire sales process and are still in front of you after the objections, then you need to start reading the signals and drawing the conversation to an outcome. How to do this will of course be further explored later in this chapter. A lack of closing shows a lack of confidence, which raises doubt in the mind of the customer. There is no shame in the act of closing the sale; there is only shame in having a conversation that unnecessarily wastes the customer's time.

FEAR OF REJECTION

Many sales opportunities have been left unclosed due to the fear of rejection. This fear is what makes many sales careers very short as people cannot tolerate a line of work that involves rejection. For a salesperson, the fear of rejection causes anxiety and can paralyse all proactive behaviour, such as prospecting and closing the sale. I vote we take a different perspective on rejection: our characters are only built through difficult times and hardship—now imagine the strength of character of a person who can endure and persevere through daily rejections.

Being rejected is not a failure on the part of the salesperson. It is a natural part of the sales process and happens to all salespeople. Rejection is a great learning experience as it can give you feedback on the quality of your presentation, your ability to uncover needs and qualify customers, and your skills in reading customers. Without rejection, how would we ever be able to assess these skills? If we never knew our flaws in these areas, we would never grow as salespeople or as communicators.

Use every customer interaction as a learning experience. In general, a humble attitude allows us to adopt a learning mode in life and we stop seeing the world in dichotomies of success and failure; rather, we see both experiences as insights for personal development.

If the rejection is around a genuine mismatch of the customer's needs and the benefits of your product, then this should be no surprise to you when it happens. Through a thorough discovery process, you will be the first to uncover this—and as such, you are in control of the level of impact that a rejection can have.

Rejection is not personal. In fact, it often can't be, because the customer might not even know you. Unless the customer is your family member, a close friend or you are an exceptionally rude person, it is not personal. It may feel personal at times because the customer is communicating to you and it is your target that will not be met, but it's not necessarily you.

So what if you do get rejected—what is the worst that could possibly happen? Will the customer point and laugh at you? Will it be like your worst teenage nightmare all over again, being rejected by your high school crush? Not likely. The worst that you will hear is 'No'. It's a word that we have heard our whole lives. It may even have been the first word that we learnt as an infant.

Remember; asking for the business is a fundamental part of our work and the customer expects it to happen. The fear is in our minds, not in reality. Let's not allow the fear of rejection to become a barrier between where we are today and greater success.

WHEN DO YOU CLOSE THE SALE?

Here is a trap that many salespeople fall into. They forget that sales is a dynamic conversation tailored to each customer, and they get into a scripted routine where they take a customer on a fixed journey that ends the presentation with a close. Each component of the conversation—or should I say *speech*—is planned out and only shifted when the customer makes a drastic comment that throws off the order.

This type of rigid routine is a stab-in-the-dark approach to selling, and the dynamics of a conversation are far more fluid that this. Even if you had the most well-constructed script, would you really wait to go through the entire spiel if the customer said, "Listen, I've been researching online and coming in to speak to salespeople over the last three weeks; I know what I want—just give me the XYC product". No need to wait, no need for a script—the customer is ready to buy.

At the other end of the spectrum are salespeople who hastily misread the customer, assume the customer is ready and desperately try to close the sale. The more times you unsuccessfully attempt to close the sale, the more challenging it becomes to recover the conversation and bring to life any rapport that has been lost. When you attempt to close when the customer is not ready, you also demonstrate to the customer that you do not care about their needs and that the sale is the most important outcome to you.

Closing the sale needs to be a natural process and expected by the customer. The time to close a sale bears no relationship with what happens in the presentation; instead, it is dependent on the readiness of the customer. So how do you know when the customer is ready to buy?

BUYING SIGNALS

Buying signals are indicators of a customer's desire to buy through the things they say or do. For every customer, their specific signal will be unique to them; however, understanding the principles of buying signals will help you understand the customer's buying temperature and advance the sales conversation.

VERBAL SIGNALS

Customers are consciously and unconsciously providing you with feedback on your sales presentation. They may use emotionally charged words and phrases like, "Fantastic," "Amazing," "Oh, that's great" or, "Hey, I really like that." These signals are easy to identify, so we need to be conscious of them and know what to do next.

Customers often make comments when they have started imagining what it is like to own your product. They may ask questions like, "Once I install it, will I be able to customise it to my settings?" or, "What is the policy on your warranty?" or, "How long does this product usually last?" The customer is visualising life with your product, which is a very positive milestone in the buying process.

Verbal buying signals also consist of questions around the logistics of the process to purchase. A customer may ask, "So when will it be installed?" or, "Will someone connect it for me or is there an instruction manual?" or, "How much does the delivery cost?" or, "Who do I call if there are issues with the installation?"

BODY LANGUAGE

The customer also shares their levels of interest to buy through their body language and facial expressions. When the customer leans forward, moves closer to you, smiles more, gives you eye contact and nods, they are showing you that they are in agreement with what you are saying and are interested to hear more.

The customer may also adjust their seat to settle in, instead of always looking like they are prepared to leave.

ACTION-BASED SIGNALS

A buying signal can also reveal itself in the things that a customer may do. When the customer grabs the brochure and starts delving into the finer details, they are indicating a greater readiness to buy. Potential clients may call a fellow decision-maker to discuss your recommendation, which in one aspect can cause difficulty as this third party has not been taken on the journey; however, it certainly shows a strong sense of willingness to buy.

It may feel unnatural and somewhat distracting to look out for all of these signals at first, but eventually it will become second nature to be able to read and interpret these behaviours. Of course, there are many signs that a customer is ready, and none of the above alone will be enough for you to be confident to close the sale. So if buying signals are only an indicator, how can we be sure that it's time to close the sale? We can't—so we need to deploy a method to determine the buying temperature.

TESTING THE WATER

Closing the sale can be likened to getting into a shower that we are not familiar with. When we step in for the first time we cautiously turn the dials; scoping out the water pressure and time for the temperature to change. Once we have done this, we are likely to put our hand in water and if that feels warm enough, more and more of the body enters the shower until we are comfortable with the temperature. This is no different to testing the customer's willingness to buy.

As discussed in the previous section, buying signals are merely indicators and not enough to determine buying behaviour alone. Using buying signals alone is like knowing the water in the shower is hot by looking at it. Sure, you see steam rising; however, your wisdom and experience still tells you to give it a trial run before jumping in and getting burnt or dealing with a cold rejection. If we test the water before jumping in, we still have time move the dials and adjust the temperature to an appropriate level.

In sales we have a similar process, except rather than using our hand to test the temperature, we use a far more sophisticated sales thermometer called the 'trial close'. The trial close is designed to test the customer's current buying temperature and determine whether the customer is ready to buy or still needs more time.

A trial close is different to close as it is not the end of the conversation and the salesperson makes it clear that there is still more to come. The purpose of a trial close is not to gain the sale, rather it is designed to elicit interest and gain feedback on your conversation so far.

Trial closing is not exclusively used at the end of the conversation or when you have run out of things to say. Trial closes should be used on a regular basis throughout your sales presentation, gaining agreement and confirmation at each stage. The last thing that you want, is to be engaging in a 30 minute conversation and, after all of that, the customer says, "Sorry, I am really confused—can you go back to the beginning?" Trial closes help you align the customers' understanding to the direction of your presentation. View this technique as a checkpoint before moving on.

Below are some simple examples of what a trial close could sound like:

- "What are your initial thoughts from what we have discussed?"

- "Based on the information we have gone through so far, how do you feel?"

- "Before we share more about ABC product, does this align with your family's needs so far?"

- "How does this sound so far?"

Did you notice the difference between the above examples and a close? Use the words 'initial thoughts', 'before we move on' and 'so far' show the customer that this not the end of the conversation and that there is more for them to learn. Some salespeople use this after explaining each benefit to guarantee that the customer has an appreciation of how their product can be helpful in its entirety.

TRIAL CLOSE OUTCOMES

Once buying signals are recognised, we confirm them with a series of trial closes before we attempt to close. In Frank Romano's *Precision Selling* he shares that a trial close can only bring one of three outcomes: *'Yes I like it,' 'No I don't'* or *'Maybe.'* Each outcome requires a different response:

YES

If the customer responds positively to your trial closes throughout the conversation, it is safe to move to the next stage of the presentation. If you hear a 'yes' both throughout and at the end of the conversation, it is safe to close the sale. This is where your approach should be fearless and assumptive. Remember; the customer has already told you a number of times that they like the product and they have demonstrated interest through buying signals and a positive response; there is no need for more closing questions. Just assume the sale.

If you ask, "So what do you want to do?" after a 'yes' response, you will only raise doubt in the customer's mind, where no doubt is required. Assumptive closing is not a pushy approach—this is you showing the customer that you are in sync with them and you have listened to them. We will discuss some techniques of assumptive closing in the following section.

NO

The way that you respond to a 'no' after a trial close is the same whether it's throughout the sales process or at the end of the conversation. Do not take this negative response as signalling the end of the conversation. If the customer has responded with a 'no', there is clearly an unspoken or unanswered objection that is holding them back. As mentioned previously, you should confidently draw out that objection in order for you to handle it and move on to remind the customer of the original benefits that appealed to them.

UNSURE/MAYBE

From experience, I can recall a number of *unsure* response types; "I need to think about it," "I'm confused," "I need more information," "I have an objection," "I need to speak to my partner." Luckily, for the salesperson, there are only two responses that can cover the above types of 'unsure'.

When responding to a "I'm unsure", the first thing that we need to do, is determine whether there is an objection or there was something unclear about what has been discussed. We can do this by asking, "When you say that you are unsure, is there something that I have been unclear about or is there something about the product that you would like to discuss further?"

If it is an objection—that is, something that they would like to discuss further—you know what to do: clarify to ensure that you have understood, and respond. If it is something that they have misinterpreted or do not understand, we need to take responsibility. Even if the customer is categorically incorrect and was not paying attention, it is still not their fault. Remember; you get paid to be engaging and they are not being paid to remain engaged. In this case we take full responsibility and say, "My apologies if I was unclear. Please let me know which part you would like me to explain in a better way." Your customers will appreciate your humility, which is far more influential than questioning the customer's intelligence or attention span.

ASSUMPTIVE CLOSE

The customer is nodding, the body language is promising and there is a supportive response to the trial close. We can now assume the sale and move on. Now, the word 'assume' in this context is not be mistaken for what was discouraged in the context of responding to objections; that is, speaking without clarifying first. This assumption has already been educated through a series of signals and trial closes.

The reason why it is important to be assumptive is out of respect to what the customer and the information they have provided you. Imagine that the customer is in agreement the whole time and have made it clear that they want the product. Would it not be time-wasting to timidly ask again for more confirmation— "Are you sure you want to go ahead with it today?". This will make us, as salespeople, seem doubtful. If we are doubtful, there is no hope for the customer to feel confident. Make the process easy and natural in a way that allows the conversation to be seamless, without all of those rigid barriers to buy.

Examples of assumptive closes:

- "The form will take three minutes to fill in and we need to start with your address."

- "For the delivery, do you prefer weekdays or weekends?"

- "We accept all forms of payment—which is the most convenient for you?"

- "Your item will be ready for you in two days—will it be you or someone else picking it up?"

Remember; this technique is not designed to trap the customer, as they always have an option to leave. It is designed to help the conversation flow and make the decision-making process easy for the customer. To support your assumptive close, it is suggested that you hold on to a compelling surprise until the end of the sale.

KEEP A SURPRISE

The sales conversation is a calculated and methodical art that cannot be spoilt by excessive excitement to tell the customer everything at once. Think of yourself as the magician who opens the show with a big-bang illusion to capture the audience, earn their respect and guarantee their engagement for the rest of the show. Each trick builds on the last and keeps them hooked. The magician of course does not waste all of their best tricks up front. Instead, they go in and out, from grand tricks, to smaller card tricks, leaving a prestigious act at the end.

The sales process is the same, except for the smoke and mirrors part. You may have two or three really compelling product benefits and some standard ones that most competitors have. The temptation is often to lay down all of your wow factors at once to show off all of the best features. The downfall in this approach is that, post the wow factors, all you have left are your standard features. When the customer is contemplating whether or not to make a buying decision, you have nothing compelling left to wow them with.

Like the magician, you need to close the sale with something up your sleeve. To determine which to share up front and which to hang on to, list out all of the benefits that you have to offer and rank them from most compelling to least. Share the number one benefit up front and save the second best until the end. This way, the customer is captivated and has a reason to stay, and you are left with a wow factor to seal the decision.

In the early 2000s, there were some luxury car dealerships that asked customers what their favourite type of music was, during the sales conversation. When approaching the close of the sale, the salesperson would surprise the customer by telling them that when they pick up the car, there will be $200 worth of CDs of their favourite genre of music for them to drive away with. Now, when buying a car worth over $100,000 a $200 value proposition seems hardly compelling; however, it closed so many sales. Why? Because it was a great surprise and wow factor that aligned with the customers' taste. $200 is not a lot of money for these customers; however, they would rarely go and purchase that many CDs in one go, so it suddenly became valuable.

LANGUAGE OF CLOSING

With this chapter focusing on closing the sale, we cannot lose sight of selling with integrity and bringing forth the new breed of salespeople who customers respond positively to. One of the worst compliments that I have ever received from a customer was, "Wow, you are a great salesperson". That was great feedback for me to realise that I had made the customer feel like they were being sold to rather than giving them an opportunity to buy. We need to be conscious of the language that we use to move it from a one-way sales presentation to a conversation.

When we use words like 'sign-up' and 'it's a deal' or when we look like we want to leave immediately after the sale, our subtitles are saying, "I got you! Smashed in another sale." This is not the final memory that you want to leave with the customer—not only because the sale is likely to cancel and referrals will be next to impossible to gain, but also because that is not the salesperson that you want to be. If your intent is always to get the sale without caring about the customer outcome, then you will not last long in this business. We need to be driven by goals beyond ourselves to sustain us.

Keep the language fun and positive, ensuring that it reflects what the customer wants, not something that you are about to do to them. You may wish to say:

- "Congratulations, you are going to save a lot of money today."

- "You should be really happy that you bought this."

- "The agreement is for 12 months on the terms that we have discussed."

- "Your family is going be to really happy when the furniture is delivered on Saturday."

All of this language shows benefits of the purchase and indicates that the customer is in control.

PATIENCE AND PERSISTENCE

Persistence and patience are often seen as opposing qualities; however, in the game of closing sales, they need to go hand-in-hand.

Traditionally, persistence is viewed as being pushy and manifests itself in never-ending conversations that can only end in a yes. Persistence that is born from the salesperson's immovable determination to get a sale poses a danger to the longevity of one's sales career. Instead, a persistence that is accompanied by patience and understanding is helpful to the customer's buying process.

This form of persistence manifests itself in the salesperson looking for many opportunities to meet the customer's need rather than persistently hammering one angle until the customer says yes. If we are getting too many 'nos' it means that we did not ask enough questions at the beginning to uncover needs—so excessively pressing the customer is not going to be effective. If they do not see value once, they will not see it the second time when nothing else has changed. It would be naïve to think that the customer has shifted their opinion without any new information.

Even the highest level of a product-flogging salesperson would feel frustrated with themselves after trying to close the sale a number of times. Don't you feel silly when you lose your phone or your remote and you find yourself looking in the same place a few times? The only difference between looking in the same place and blind persistence in sales is that you have roped someone else into the insanity.

If you find yourself stuck without any other options besides hammering the one point, go back to asking questions to uncover the customer's wants/needs, in order to draw out what the customer truly values. Successful and caring salespeople will uncover a list of matches between the customer's perception of value and the benefits of the product. Go through that list with the customer to remind them of the reasons this will benefit them.

On the other hand, if there is no matched value that you can identify with the customer, then why are you persistently trying to close the sale? Neither you nor the customer is ready to close the deal.

KNOWING WHEN TO GIVE UP

This book does not have the silver bullet of selling—because there isn't one. A wise salesperson knows when to persist and when to give up. Like buying signals, we should also be accustomed to reading exit signals—i.e., when the customer wants to leave the conversation. Some salespeople preach that 'Three nos means go'—however, I am not that superstitious. Use your intuition, experience and common sense.

Observe their facial expression and body language (which always reveals the truth). Listen to what they what they are saying, and further experience with your target market will guide you the rest of the way.

CREATING URGENCY

We explored the idea of urgency in the 'no hurry' objection in the previous chapter, and will address it again with the lens of closing the sale.

Many years ago, an experienced salesperson joined my business and was out there selling subscription television. After a few days of no results, I went out and observed what he was saying to customers. His pitch went something like this: "Excuse me, madam, I am here to inform you that over the next seven days, there is a convoy of trucks coming into your suburb and one in every seven houses will be given a satellite to get access to subscription television. It will be a free installation if you hurry and subscribe now." People's reaction? They either laughed at him or told him how confused they were, as they had been living in the suburb for years and never saw a convoy of trucks coming… because they weren't.

Many salespeople attempt to create urgency to help close the sale; however, often it is just a tactic rather than a genuine benefit to the customer to act now. They will falsely create scarcity by saying, "This is the last one we have in stock" or, "If you don't get it now, another customer might come and buy it." I am sure that at times this is true—however, in most instances, it is not. When a salesperson says, "This is our last one in stock," I wonder what they generally do when stock runs out—do they just wait until the whole store is empty? What would they do if the customer said, "I wanted to buy 10 of them"? Would the salesperson's response be, "Sorry you can't buy 10—we only have one"? Of course not. The salesperson magically taps in to tap into their source of inventory—whether it is be in a storage room or another store.

This false sense of urgency has given salespeople a bad reputation and made customers disbelieve in the slightest glimmering of the tactic. On the other hand, there is no doubt that creating urgency advances the sales process by assisting the customer in making a decision. So how do we do it in an honest and effective way?

Simple: do the opposite of what the traditional salesperson does; that is, create a compelling sense of urgency which motivates the customer into action by ensuring that it is real/honest, centred around the customer—not the organisation—and satisfies the question, 'Why should I buy now?'

Below are a few techniques and examples that meet the above requirements:

CONTINUE THINKING

"Miss Customer, you mentioned that you have been thinking about buying this for six months. Now that you have a subject matter expert in front you, feel free to share your thoughts and ask any questions. If you don't, you may spend another six months thinking about it."

This type of urgency is putting the control back in the customer's hands and sharing a reality about their buying behaviour. It also reminds the customer of the opportunity to clear all of their thoughts and questions with the expert available.

POWER OF OWNING IT NOW

"I cannot decide for you when you should buy it; instead, what I can do is ask what it would mean to you to set up the TV in your house tonight instead of waiting a few more weeks? That is why you came into the store, isn't it?"

Reminding them of the joys of *now* creates excitement in the place of pressure. Also, you want to remind customers that they did not just invest all of this time to leave their house, come into the store and have a long conversation with a salesperson if there was not some degree of readiness to buy.

LONGER BENEFIT

"You mentioned that your long-term goal is to buy a house, and therefore opening this investment account today will help speed up that process as you can start earning interest from today."

Similar to the *power of owning it now*, however, this form of urgency is relevant when your product has an accumulated benefit—that is, buying the product now would kick-start a series of benefits to the customer.

QUICKLY ALLEVIATING A PAIN

"The benefit of joining our phone plan today is that you can immediately stop paying too much with your current provider."

Placing urgency around alleviating the customer's pain, if said with the right levels of authenticity and compassion, will be interpreted as helping and not selling. The customer will be able to perceive your genuine concern, and greater levels of trust will be built, which brings confidence in the decision-making process.

Did you notice how none of the above statements/questions were centred around a time-limited offer? These types of tactics only demonstrate the shortcomings of your organisation and will be lost on the customer. I am not suggesting that you don't tell when an offer runs out, rather do not make this a point of pressure where the customer is forced to make a hasty decision.

WHERE NEXT?

As the author of this book, I am very grateful that you have made it this far, and I will take this as feedback that these pages have added value to you in your sales journey. The following chapter is about sales management in the context of leading people that want to succeed in sales by being not having to change their values. It is for current and aspiring leaders or people who want to help influence the environment in which they work. If this is for you, keep reading.

If you do not fit into any of these categories, I encourage you to skip ahead and read the final chapter about *Continuous Learning*, which will share some simple advice on how to keep growing and developing your sales skills.

9 SALES LEADERSHIP

Managing salespeople, team dynamics, business outcomes and culture can be a tough gig—however, it is a vital role in the dynamics of this ever-changing environment. The greater challenge that readers of this book may be facing is that they are working with salespeople who do not instinctively value the art of selling and are currently unhappy with their profession or feel they do not fit. These challenges will not be taken lightly in the upcoming sections, and as leaders, we will need to adopt some fresh mindsets first, to create a platform in which teams can advance.

This chapter cannot cover and do justice to all topics of sales management—nor is it intended to; rather, we will focus on the areas that matter most to those who do not see themselves as salespeople.

SORRY BOSS, I AM NOT A SALESPERSON

As a sales manager, you will be confronted by this comment—as I have in my own career. The content within the previous chapters addressed this topic; however, from a leadership lens, we should be mindful of useful attitudes and qualities that help in handling this conversation.

It is important to be sensitive and recognise the journey that the salesperson has come on. This won't be difficult as you can reflect on your own feelings starting out in the frontline. When working with a major bank, I witnessed a group of management consultants from a highly reputable firm get this very wrong. There was a large push to get mortgage lenders to start proactively prospecting through a new sales training. In the workshop, it taught them how to prepare for a cold sales call, plan through targeted mapping, identify qualified leads and make a pitch. The expectation was for the lenders to head out on the road, approach businesses and ask to speak to their employees, to offer them a deal on a home loan.

After a number of attempts to train, coach and instruct these lenders, it was a resounding flop and it galvanised very few people into action. During the diagnosis, the consultants were quick to label the mortgage lenders as lazy, unmotivated and stubborn. Of course none of these were true as they were extremely hard-working, driven and open people. What the consultants were not doing is appreciating the journey these lenders had been on. If they had attempted to do this, they would have been able to acknowledge that 10 years previous to this intervention, most of these lenders would have started in an entry-level role within the bank as a teller. That role is highly inbound, where customers will line up, make a request and you fulfil. At most you may suggest products or services, but nothing beyond that. After serving time in that role, you would be promoted into a sales role where you are fulfilling more complex sales in yet another inbound environment. Customers are directed to you and you fulfil their request and cross-sell. Years later, you become a lender in an exclusive office and again people walk in and request to see you.

Their organisation had dedicated 10 or so years to building a habit and routine around an inbound approach to sales—and then suddenly we expect to unwind all of that in a two-hour workshop about how to prospect. Previous to this, no training had been conducted to assist these salespeople to develop their prospecting skills. Instead, they put them in a room, set them up for failure and called lazy.

Building capacity in an individual is a process, not a two-hour event. If you want your team to shift from service to sales or inbound to outbound, you need to observe the preceding chapters, starting with mindset and working up to skills.

Despite the temptation or pressure from senior management, in some organisations, we know that the answer is not to fire them all and start again with cut-throat salespeople. Don't forget that customer-loving, service-oriented people make great salespeople. We need to work with them at their pace and help them succeed by capitalising on their own strengths and not just fixing their weaknesses.

TAKING RESPONSIBILITY FOR OTHER PEOPLE'S RESULTS

One of the greatest mindset challenges of a sales leader is the idea of being one step removed from the result. Essentially, you are responsible for the actions of others. Many would say that this is the same in all kinds of leadership and management functions; however, I feel that the variability in sales performance magnifies this challenge for sales leaders.

When managing a team of business analysts to an outcome, you will still have challenges of laziness, incompetence and poor conduct; however, the process and outcomes are more controlled. If outcomes for an analyst are not met, often we can extend the timeline, rather than piling on more outcomes. In sales, we are relying on the dynamics between a salesperson and a customer actually working, the customer being a qualified opportunity, and there being a need—before the sales process has even begun. Also, the income and growth of your business relies on the ability of a salesperson to perform their role.

The challenge of being removed from direct results is also perpetuated by the fact that, when results are above target, salespeople get the praise from senior management, and when sales are low, the sales leader is the one who gets disciplined.

The story is not all doom and gloom for the sales leader, as these are just mindsets that can be shifted. Firstly, yes, we are responsible for the results even though we did not create them. In the same way, when you continue climbing the hierarchy of the organisation, you are still responsible for results and you can definitely impact them. Just because we do not directly create a result, it does not mean that we cannot control them. Think of it like this: if you wanted to, do you think you could slow down sales? Of course you can—it would be quite simple. You could easily lower the morale, misdirect people, avoid coaching, be unfair,

161

encourage long breaks and distract the focus of the salespeople. The inverse of these actions can also be drivers that increase sales.

This book is not suggesting that sales leaders have various degrees of control; it is explicitly saying that *they have total control*. Put the world's most inspiring and skilled sales leader in the same environment with the same team who had a poor leader, and there would be different results. This logic demonstrates that when sales are up or down, the way that a sales leader can impact them is the same way a salesperson does. Reflect, build your skills and act.

Also, the notion of not being recognised when the team performs and being scolded when results are low is part and parcel of the challenges of leadership. Do you not think that the lack of public recognition is an indicator of how senior leaders feel about you? Remember; in a lot of circumstances your manager has also led a team of salespeople and they understand the work that you have done. Take pride in your sales team, rejoice in their recognition and take responsibility for their results.

FROM SALES TO MANAGEMENT

Ram Charan et al. describes in the book *The Leadership Pipeline* that, as we advance through the various stages of leadership (manage self, manage others, manage managers, functional manager, business manager and group manager), there are three things that we need to change each time. These are our *skills, time application* and *values*. Let's dig deeper on moving from a salesperson to a sales leader.

SKILLS

When you become a manager, your sales skills are no longer your primary super power. Although important, these skills are trumped by your need to get others to sell. A fundamental skill is that of coaching and teaching. Before we assume that we have an agreed definition of coaching and teaching, let's discuss the difference and why we need to be good at both.

A teacher is like your maths teacher at school. They have superior skills to their students and could beat them in every exam. They role-model the behaviour, and students admire the knowledge of their teacher and learn from them. A coach, on the other hand, does not need to be better than the people whom he/she is coaching. For example, an Olympic swimming coach does need to jump in the pool and beat the world record to help the swimmer understand swimming. Instead, the coach is able to stand at the side of the pool, observe the swimmer and coach them on the most minor errors that the athlete would never see themselves.

In the game of sales management, we need to be both. As banking executive Nate Fosnaugh once said, we need to be a 'teaching coach'. You need to observe your people on a regular basis and help them improve on their sales skills. You can see the intricate things that even the most self-actualised salesperson will not be able to observe on their own—and you can help them overcome these. Where sales differs from Olympic swimming lies in the fact that inspiration is drawn from the coach's ability to be like the teacher—and to jump in front of the customer and own the conversation. There is nothing more demotivating for a salesperson than to see his or her manager fail at the game they preach.

Most sales leaders have come from a sales background, so, initially, people will have that respect for you, as they have seen you succeed. Despite sales being a secondary skill for a leader, we will still need to maintain this by sharpening the axe and staying close to the action.

TIME APPLICATION

How you spend your time need to change when you take on a leadership role. Your application of time will shift from getting sales and spending the majority of time with customers, to coaching others. Your priorities shift from your tasks to assisting the tasks of your team.

These new responsibilities do not divorce you completely from the sales action, as discussed above. Make sure that you put some customer-facing time in your diary, to ensure you keep coaching relevant to the current environment. The time you spend selling will be a cause of inspiration to your team; however, an excess of this can be seen as you not growing as a leader, or neglecting your team. Additionally, overdoing sales time creates negative feelings towards a sales leader as the team may think:

- Why are they getting paid more to do the same work?

- My manager takes all of my sales opportunities.

- I wish they spent more time coaching me instead of taking the commission.

In general, a sales leader will have less time doing and more time planning. A lot this will initially feel unproductive as it is not directly leading to sales. This is why we need to shift our work values.

VALUES

In this context, 'values' should not be mistaken for life values such as love for ones family and following a set of high moral standards. These values are not expected to change due to a promotion at work; instead, we should see these as work values and things that we hold as important in our jobs. These could range from tasks to standards, to an ethos that drives performance.

On many occasions, we see sales managers who believe that it is important to get in there and always be number one on the league ladder to show the team how it's done. This value should shift to working with others and advancing collectively. It does not matter how fast you can run—what matters when you are a manager is that you can move at a pace that aligns with your team, and can help them advance to greater speeds. Only when the whole team is advancing will you see progress in performance, culture and productivity in your sales business. Also, logically this is not a good move for a sales manager, as we know that, no matter how many sales you get on your own, it will never equate to the result of a collective effort—if this were the case, it would mean that you are still a salesperson and not a manager.

You need to shift from a competing mindset to one of collaboration, and move from celebrating your personal victories to rejoicing in the success of others.

SELF-AWARENESS

Self-awareness is one of the first cognitive milestones towards sales mastery. As a leader you must role-model this and know how to bring it out of others.

Feedback, coaching and skill development will be increasingly difficult the longer we hold off attempts to bring our teams to a strong state of awareness. People will become defensive and confused which will never galvanise the salesperson into change. There will be varying degrees of self-awareness capability within your team; however, the vision is for us to be so proficient in our own awareness that we are able to step outside of our own situation and view ourselves from a third-person point of view. A third-person view is objective, honest and has no emotional attachments. When you dissociate from yourself you are able to critique yourself and work towards self-development.

How many times do we meet someone who has a misalignment between the perception of themselves and reality? If we are not self-aware and don't know what to change about ourselves, others will do it for us and tell us how to act. If we want our non-salesy teams to succeed in sales by maintaining their character, they need to know their own character. If we tell our unaware teams to become salespeople, they will naturally emulate the first thing that they see—which is likely to a cut-throat style of selling.

The more coaching we do with our teams, the more aware they become, as their capability to discuss their own performance grows. In a competitive environment, it is common that people will refrain from openly sharing their faults. The only way that this culture will change is when the leader is role-modelling a high level of awareness. As a leader, it is important to show humility in your success and show openness in your errors. Admitting error does not imply weakness; it shows maturity through learning. We need to move away from a culture that labels vulnerability as a weakness, and instead promote this a sign of self-awareness and emotional intelligence. Making the same mistake over and over due to arrogantly hiding from failure, on the other hand, demonstrates the opposite.

COACHING

Coaching is a fundamental skill for a sales leader. Your skills of observation, your understanding of sales and communication principles will be paramount in this endeavour. The topic of coaching is so detailed that it is deserving of a series of books on its own, and this volume does not attempt to do it complete justice. Rather, we will touch on a few common errors that sales managers make in coaching and how we can avoid them.

In many sales cultures, coaching is seen as a punishment. This is not explicitly spoken about; however, people associate coaching with poor sales performance, time-wasting and embarrassment. If this is the case in your business, this is symptomatic of a few sales management ills—but, believe me, there's a cure.

PREPOSITIONING A COACHING SESSION

When you walk a team member into your office, sit them down, close the door and commence a coaching session, the sales agent has a few questions running through their mind: "Why are we having a coaching session?", "What have I done wrong?" and "Am I in trouble?"

These are natural feelings based on previous experiences and war stories from colleagues. The good news is that we already know the answers to these questions—therefore, it is important that we strongly preposition the purpose and outcomes of the coaching session before the questions are asked. To answer the question "why are we having a coaching session?", be specific and honest. There are many reasons a coaching conversation may take place: skill gap observations, new product launches, fulfilment of ongoing development plans and/or a new sales process.

You also want to dispel any negative associations with coaching and share with the team member that they are not in trouble and have not done anything wrong. Any first-time error that a salesperson makes should not be punished—rather, it should be seen as an area for development. We need to turn stumbling blocks to stepping stones and view each weakness as an area for development. If we show little faith in a person's abilities to develop and grow, then there is no hope for them.

Being evaluated on your sales skills can be nerve-racking as it is a direct reflection on your communication and human relations skills. Since sales skills are synonymous to life skills, any type of constructive feedback can easily feel like a personal attack—if it is not prepositioned carefully. Your team member needs to know that you genuinely care about them and that their development is important.

Sales leaders also need to separate an individual's behaviour from their identity. It is similar to childhood education principles, where we do not discourage the individual, only the behaviour. Coaches need to be conscious of the language being used when having these conversations.

In your preposition of a coaching conversation, sharing what the coaching is for is as important as sharing what the coaching is not for—that is, telling the salesperson that coaching is not about criticism of them; it is not a forum to blame others and it is not designed to catch people making mistakes so that you can prove you are smarter than them.

Putting this all together, a preposition may sound like:

> "Emily, as a part of the ongoing development and growth of the team, I wanted to spend more time on coaching with everyone. Coaching will not be sporadic and overly reactionary. Instead, we want to set large goals with regard to your development, and each coaching session will be an incremental milestone leading towards your desired state.
>
> Throughout the session, we will discuss some of the findings from observed performance. This will be a two-way conversation and any feedback given, whether it be complimentary or constructive, is solely for your benefit and with your development in mind. This is not a space for criticism or excessive justification.
>
> It is important that we adopt a mode of learning and take this opportunity to accelerate your development and get closer to where you want to be."

KEEP IT REGULAR

As mentioned earlier, coaching is a core part of a sales leader's role and not something performed only when times are tough.

When someone is performing well, coaching will take them to the next level. Coaching conversations must be regular and progressive. Each coaching session must build on the last and the topics will naturally grow in complexity as the salesperson continues to develop their skills.

When coaching becomes a part of your operating rhythm, your prepositions will not be as elaborate, as it becomes an expected norm.

BITE-SIZED INFORMATION

Learning about gaps in your conversation skills can be overwhelming, and implementing changes to them can be difficult for most people. As a great coach, you may have the ability to observe all performance gaps and micro skills that a salesperson can improve on. We should refrain from sharing all of our observations, and instead use our wisdom to prioritise the one overarching skill that encompasses a number of errors and will generate the best improvement. When you look through the list that you may have written down, it should become obvious to you which is the most important.

I witnessed a manager have a three-hour coaching session with a staff member, going through a long list of observations about the person's skill gaps. The recipient of the coaching approached me afterward and mentioned that they were so confused about where to start and what to do next—so they did nothing. The only result of this meeting was that the staff member started to become distant from his manager and applied lip service to keep him off his back. This led to more negative associations with coaching.

Sharing an entire set of observations with the salesperson is very tempting, and even I have fallen victim to this trap. Some time ago, in an observation session with a salesperson, I wrote two and a half pages' worth of notes on what he needed to do to improve. I knew that going through them all would not be effective, so I looked through the list and identified one skill that he could develop which would dramatically improve his results. When he glanced at my page and saw the extensiveness of my list, he begged me to just list his problem areas and promised not be overwhelmed. He told me that he was passionate about his development and would make his own plan.

I knew that this was a bad idea and, after going back and forth explaining why I didn't want to do that, I went against my judgement and showed him the list. Before I even started reading from it, I could see that it took the wind out of him. It was like a kick in the guts seeing how many gaps he had. After that moment, each coaching session was an emotional challenge for him.

We must deliver feedback and coaching in bite-sized pieces so that the idea can be easily digested by the recipient. Never make the mistake that I did and give into the desperate pleads of a salesperson wanting to know more. They will claim it is good for their awareness and development—when in fact it does more damage than good. Coaching should not demolish and rebuild a person; instead, it is like renovating a home one room at a time. Give them one skill to work on, go into depth, give them a chance to practise and make it a habit. Once they have reached an acceptable level of competency on this, you can comfortably move on to the next skill.

COACHING IS BASED ON FACTS, NOT OPINIONS

Coaching conversations can sometimes end in long-drawn-out debates between the opinion of the staff member and the opinion of the coach—particularly when the salesperson lacks self-awareness. These differing opinions are either settled by one outranking the other, or by agreeing to disagree. I witnessed a leader speak to a new staff member, referring to them as arrogant and condescending to their teammates. Naturally, the staff member asked for a real example and the response was, "I don't have an example; it's just a feeling that I am getting. It's more a vibe than anything else." As you can imagine, this erupted into a time-consuming and counterproductive argument that drew a further distance between the leader and their team member.

Coaching interventions need to be based on facts and not opinions. Facts can be drawn from personal observations or from outcomes viewed in sales reports. Stray from using the opinions of others as these can be easily debated. To avoid these back-and-forth debates, ensure that accounts of the development area are very specific and indisputable. This is not to trap the team member, but rather to move away from defensive behaviour/excuses and focus on their development.

In a performance conversation I had with one of my team members, we reviewed her self-assessment where she had described herself as a role model in team work. My assessment was that she still required a lot of development in this space—and there was no way that I was going to enter into a debate or create an environment where she needed to get defensive. She was asked to explain the reasons why she saw herself as a role model, and I listened attentively. When she was finished, I shared in a kind and caring way that I didn't recognise role-modelling in her current behaviour, prepared with five examples of where she did not demonstrate this behaviour with the dates, times and other surrounding information. After moving into the second example, she quickly acknowledged and spent a moment reflecting on those incidents. Then, with the most resourceful attitude, she responded with, "So how can I get better and make sure that this doesn't happen again next year?"

Two-Way Conversation

Effective coaching is as much about telling as it is listening. It is a two-way conversation that involves mutual contribution.

Involving your staff members in the conversation is not merely a token gesture to appease their ego. Rather, it is fundamental to the coaching session as your diagnosis of a *skill or will* gap can never be complete until you have heard their point of view. Create a space where the recipient of the coaching session feels comfortable in your presence and wants to express themselves. Do not cut them off or dismiss their comments, as this will stifle their development and place them in a non-resourceful state.

Start every session by asking them to share their thoughts on their performance, and if they are struggling to express themselves, ask more questions to allow them to articulate it better. Continue to ask questions, keeping them engaged. They should never feel like a passive audience member, as their role is integral to the success of the coaching session.

Your ability to coach an individual will be vastly enhanced by the strength of their self-awareness. Providing more opportunities for them to express their perception of themselves will certainly strengthen their ability to self-assess more accurately.

UNDERSTANDING VS. ADVANCEMENT

When endeavouring to train someone, we often assess the effectiveness of our endeavour with the idea of guaranteeing that they understand every part of it and are able to reach mastery. This is an unfair way to view your people, as everyone has started on a different point on the continuum of learning and absorbs information at various paces. It is expected that some will advance beyond the text of the learning at great speed, while others will be stuck on basic concepts.

Rather than being obsessed with people reaching true depths of understanding, we should mark our success in terms of people advancing in understanding. If individuals are growing and getting better, that is a coaching achievement. If someone learns at a slower pace, they may only take on one extra piece of information. As a coach, we should remain detached from immediate outcomes and allow people to grow at a pace that is consistent with their capacity to grow.

When we view people like this, it shapes the way we manage them and recognise their work. We see them for their unique strengths and are patient with their poor performance.

REACHING NEW LEVELS OF UNDERSTANDING

An uncommonly used lever in sales management is motivating people through learning. Traditionally, we associate learning with boredom, classrooms and paternalistic teaching environments— however, it does not need to be like that. People get very stale in their jobs when they are not learning anything new or advancing in their current understanding of topics. To maintain a high-performance sales culture, it is critical that regular learning is a part of that.

Observe your team and avoid dichotomous viewpoints such as, "I have high performers and low performers; there are smart people and not-smart people." Instead, it is more useful to view individuals from the point of view that they are on a learning continuum and are all advancing. If a staff member has a superficial understanding of rapport-building, instead of labelling them as *stupid* it may be more useful to share a deeper understanding of rapport. This will not only advance their performance, but will motivate them as they are working in an environment in which they are growing.

In helping salespeople reach new levels of understanding, leaders also need to be myth busters. Similar to how salespeople bust customer myths, managers need to do the same with their team. As a salesperson, when you are neck-deep in customer complaints and questions, it is difficult to step back and view your situation objectively. Fortunately, sales managers have the luxury of an objective balcony view of their environment and can respond to untrue comments that their team are making.

Common myths include, 'Not all customers are interested,' 'We've already saturated the market,' 'This offer doesn't work,' and, 'I am not a salesperson'. To bust these myths, we can draw on the 'Know, Believe, Express' methodology outlined in Chapter 3. Make sure that you respond with facts, not opinions, and persist until your team member believes it and can confidently express the view to others.

MOTIVATION AND SHIFTING HABITS

If not being proactive and enthusiastic forms a part of the salesperson's habit, it will be hard to shake off. There are many theories to habit change such as, 'It takes 21 days to change a habit', 'If you see it seven times, you know the habit has formed' or '90 days embeds behaviours'. There may be science behind these theories of habit change; however, experience has shown that there are inconsistencies across different people. Setting a definitive number on habit change is ignoring the unpredictable nature of human beings.

Habit change is dependent on a person's motivation to change and self-discipline to sustain the change. You need to ensure that there is enough leverage for the person to act. People who are not your typical salesperson will refrain from telling you that money is a motivator or enough leverage to cause a behaviour change—

whether it is true or not. A high level of achievement may not be a big motivator either, as the idea of smashing in sales will not inspire these individuals.

This new breed of salespeople will often respond to more altruistic outcomes that remind them of the nobility of their profession, rather than the selfish outcomes that they can achieve. Use this as a motivator, not a guilt-trip. We do not want to start every coaching conversation with, "Think about all of the customer needs you neglected". Remind them of the opportunity available to help each of their customers and solve their problems. If this motivator is strong, ensure you keep your language consistent and don't let it drop. When you check in with the salesperson, don't ask how many sales they got; ask how many problems were solved. Encourage their noble desires and develop this strength, as it is powerful and sustainable in a lengthy sales career.

How long does this habit last, on average? This habit will stop when it no longer becomes important to you. As a leader, your words cast a long shadow, whether you think you are influential or not. You cannot afford to rely on rigid numerical theories about habit change—if you want behavioural change, you observe it until you want it to stop. You must continue to drive the behaviour until it is no longer important, and if you stop talking about a certain topic, it will no longer be important to the salesperson. You can drive change with your team; however, do not aim for habit change—aim for genuine and personalised motivation. If you've nailed that, then habit will willingly follow.

In an environment of non-salespeople, it is critical that leaders create a culture that encourages high performance, continuous learning and motivation to stay. Behavioural change cannot be sustained without a strong culture to support it, and we know that sales will not grow without behavioural flexibility and strong staff engagement. According to the research conducted by Bluewolf in *The Essential Guide to Customer Obsession*, "An engaged employee closes 33% more deals". The following sections will explore some elements of a thriving sales culture.

REWARD AND RECOGNITION

There is nothing more demotivating than working hard, putting in your blood, sweat and tears and not being recognised. Reward and recognition are a critical part of a high-performing sales culture. We know that people want to feel appreciated and they want to know that their work has been valued. This will confirm past actions and galvanise future endeavours.

Debates between monetary rewards and non-monetary rewards can often waste time and miss the point all together. There is a place for both of these, as people like money and people want to hear *Thank you*. At the end of each day, I make the effort of thanking the individuals in my team by simply saying, "Thank you for all of your work today." As Seth Godin outlines in his book *Linchpin*, we should treat employees like volunteers and acknowledge that they are getting paid to do their tasks, but they volunteer their gifts, their talents, their creative ideas and enthusiasm. Whether a reward is monetary or not is not an overwhelming concern; rather, the reward needs to drive performance by being clear, public and consistent.

MAKE REWARDS CLEAR

It is important that we define what we wish to recognise. If we only reward the outcome, then someone's uplift in sales, high-performance improvement or personal development may never be recognised. Rewarding improvement in outcomes is very important, as people are often not self-actualised enough to know how they achieved above their norm, so if they want to repeat it again, they may not know how. At the other end of the spectrum, rewarding behaviours alone can mask poor results. Which is why we need a balance of rewards based on outcomes and those on driving behaviours.

Ensure that there is clarity on what will be rewarded—these should not be surprises, as everyone needs to be aware of where they stand. Make it clear, for example, that you want everyone to increase their conversion rates from conversation to sale before surprising them with an award.

RECOGNISE PUBLICLY

Make recognition public and known to others. Secret prizes here and there do not benefit the recipient or others. If you have asked your team to stretch their performance and someone achieves this, it should be shouted from the roof tops. A significant portion of the benefits of recognising performance are the impacts that it has on those who are watching and are motivated to be rewarded next.

BE CONSISTENT AND FAIR

Reward measures need to be fair and consistent across all staff to maintain motivation. Everyone needs to feel like they have a chance to win.

As with everything that we do, we should remember to apply the rules of moderation—and there is such a thing as too much recognition. I know this as I have fallen into this trap in the past. Some time ago, I managed a team of business development managers and sales coaches where I used to motivate them by focusing on their positive qualities. A small step for them was reciprocated with a giant leap of recognition. This over-the-top and excessive amount of recognition created dependencies and disillusionment.

The one day that I dropped the ball and recognised one staff member for a certain action and not another, I never heard the end of it. My team's performance had become dependent on excessive recognition and its absence stifled progress and performance. Disillusionment about one's performance was also caused when it came to performance reviews, despite the fact that I conducted weekly catch-ups where I openly spoke about their performance, including development areas. This overly celebrated environment caused them to rate themselves as *'top performers'*, which brought them shock when they heard otherwise.

An overuse of recognition can also weaken the power of your message. If you tell someone that you are *'blown away'* by their performance every day, what do you say when they have gone above and beyond that? You might say it's the most amazing thing that you have ever seen—and then what? There will be a point where the English language will not suffice to boost the human ego, and then you are stuck saying the same thing over and over again. Sincerity and power is lost, and then the good intent behind the recognition is wasted.

Set clear performance standards and milestones of reward and don't waver from this.

FEAR OF BEING NUMBER ONE

In a non-typical sales environment, where reward and recognition have not been established, people may not aspire to be number one. I met a lady who had been working for the same company for over 20 years, and when I asked her, "Do you want to be the number one salesperson?" she responded with, "No way!" Slightly confused and curious, I asked, "What about number two?" to which she responded, "Yeah, I could feel comfortable with that"

It blew my mind to hear that some feared being the best, but they were comfortable to be second best. So what does this tell us? After digging deeper and speaking with others who related to these feelings, there was a notion that being number one implied a great deal of pressure from management and created enemies within the team.

This is symptomatic of a culture that has fallen victim to tall-poppy syndrome—a term that describes how people who have generated success will be cut down, resented and condemned. This does not just relate to the workplace; we see it in sports, where overly successful teams are cut down at any cost and, adversely, the success of underdogs calls for celebration.

As a leader, we cannot allow this culture to continue and we must create an environment where success is applauded. We need to avoid placing too much emphasis on the outcome and focus our attention on the level of effort that was made to achieve such a result. Ensure that winners do not boast and create enemies, but also give them their time in the sun to be recognised by their peers. This is a tricky one and my only advice is to observe it, be aware and encourage people to rejoice in the success of others.

TAKING NUMBERS SERIOUSLY

Sales leaders are traditionally great with people, but are not lovers of accounting, metrics, analysis and paperwork. This is another important shift from sales to leadership: sales managers need to get obsessed with statistics. Well-presented and accurate numbers can serve as guidance to leaders. They will show you the drivers for success and the gaps in your performance. They will direct coaching decisions. Data objectifies our perception of reality as they cannot be denied and they dissipate arguments and excuse-driven anecdotes.

As I walk off my statistical soapbox, I think you get the point. Sales leaders need to be aware of the specific metrics that drive success in your team. So often I see leaders consumed by reports and numbers that do not contribute to more sales. They may be doing excessive comparisons looking at the results of others or benchmarking themselves against their year-to-date or half-year-to-date performance. Data should not be exclusively used for retrospective reporting in which we indulge our ego by looking at previous results that we can yell out in our next sales meeting. So then what?

We need to view data as a tool for planning. If we cannot act on the data, then often it is a waste of time looking at it. As David McCandless, author of *Information is Beautiful* once put it, "data is soil not oil". This tells me that the numbers are not an end in themselves or some rich currency that we have, rather a means to get an outcome and grow our businesses.

If we take on this lens, we can see that numbers must lead to clear actions. Whether it be offer management, resource alignment or coaching, we make sure that our decisions are based on facts and not only on our subjective perceptions of reality.

INSPIRATION

To sustain enthusiasm and maintain a strong team vision, sales leaders need to inspire their teams. By 'inspiration', one is not referring to a short-term excitement based on charismatic speakers or heartfelt videos—although they can work for the short term. In this context, inspiration is born from connecting a team member's values to the work of the organisation.

If someone values their contribution to others, then their leader needs to connect the work that they are doing to the contribution of others. As a sales leader you can say, "Imagine how many more customers you would be able to help if you were able to demonstrate the value of our products in a clearer sequence."

If the salesperson values career progression, you can say

"Let's help you get that interview for the next management role, by showing how you share learning with other team members."

In general, people who work in the frontline of the business want to know that their work is significant and contributes to the big picture. Nobody wants to believe that their work is superficial as people want to leave a legacy—whether it be something simple they did for a customer or a large-scale initiative for the organisation. When your organisation announces record profits or an above-plan result, congratulate your team and logically connect their efforts, no matter how relatively small, to this result. This gives your team something bigger to aspire to than their own results. We don't need to wait for a significant moment to remind them of this. Remind people on a regular basis why it is worth coming into work.

Inspiration is not limited to your words, but also involves your actions. Ask yourself, are people inspired by you? If so, are people inspired by the *work you do* or your *leadership*? There is a difference. Certain leaders adopt the value of needing to show their staff that they are better than them. To an extent, your ability to perform their work is inspirational; however, as discussed in a previous section an overemphasis on this can be disempowering and eventually become the cause of resentment. We sometimes assume that great managers are those who *always* get involved or get their hands dirty. No—it's inspiring to know that you have a manager who is willing to get their hands dirty and not necessarily do it all the time. Work-based inspiration must be drawn from your leadership. People become inspired by excellent leaders who can establish a high-performance culture and bring people together to work towards a common vision.

Lead the ship from the front rather than scrubbing the deck faster than everyone else.

'GIVING AN A'

Andrew Carnegie, who was one of the wealthiest men in our history, boasted having forty-three millionaires working for him. When asked how he hired forty-three millionaires, he responded with, "None of them were millionaires when I hired them. Developing people is like mining for gold. When you mine for gold, you expect to sift through piles of dirt to find one speck of gold, but not once are you focussing on the dirt."

To 'give an A' is a brilliant concept developed by Rosamund and Benjamin Zander and presented in the book *The Art of Possibility*. Benjamin Zander is a conductor and well-known music teacher who uses this concept in his classes. At the beginning of each year, Zander tells his class, "Your grade is an A". He prefaces this grade with a condition, which is that each student must write a letter dated the following year saying, "Dear Mr Zander, I got my A because…" and then they complete the letter by describing the person that they will become, who of course deserved that 'A'. When Zander reads that letter, he makes a commitment to treat people as they had described themselves in that letter.

This profound teaching approach is born from a philosophy on how we should treat others. Zander recognises nobility and greatness in others and creates an environment where these great qualities can come out. When we teach someone or coach them in a skill, we are not injecting the skill in them, nor are we creating the skill out of nowhere. Instead, we are bringing to life skills and talents that are latent with people and showing them how to use them.

This rule does not mean that we must agree with people's behaviours even if they are negative. *Giving an A* implies that if the person has nine bad qualities and one good one, then we should focus on the one good one and help them grow.

10 CONTINUOUS LEARNING

Congratulations—you have made it to the end of the book. Now, reading this book is one step among many towards sales success. It would be misleading of me to tell you that one book alone is enough learning to sustain a healthy sales career. This requires a mature, curious mindset structured around continuous learning.

A LEARNING MINDSET

To be successful in sales, we need to be active students of the game and not just passive bystanders. There are very few timeless sales methods, and we always need to take a step outside of day-to-day routines and objectively critique our own performance.

Be strategic about your learning and work through a cycle of action, reflection, training and more action. Knowledge that is not embedded in action does nothing more than indulge the ego. We need to test the gold with fire by using what we learn and then immediately reflecting on it. See yourself like a world-class swimmer who jumps in the pool, does a few laps and steps out for immediate feedback from their coach. Once you have learnt about your next steps, do not hesitate another moment before jumping back in the pool. This is what a master in sales does.

Be persistent and active in your pursuit for knowledge and passionately seek understanding. Be smart and abandon methods that are not working. Avoid defensive behaviours and, when someone is giving you feedback, listen, learn and apply. A mature learner is comfortable with feedback and does not shy away from role plays.

Don't subscribe to one way of thinking; be open and flexible to change your opinions—as they could be wrong. I have met many salespeople and sales trainers who cannot waver from the methodology that they have been taught and refuse to learn another way. Be prepared to unlearn habits and comforts. A good learner has a strong discipline to perform the right behaviours every day and not slip back into old habits. Remember; sales, communication and human relations are life skills—use your sales skills inside and outside the arena of sales. Don't have a sales persona and then a social persona—this what the traditional cheesy salespeople do. Be consistent. Be the same person in sales and your personal life. Consistency builds trust from your friends and your customers.

Keep your long-term goals in mind and view your most uncomfortable learning experiences as critical stepping stones to a sustainable career. "Education can be expensive. Ignorance can cost you more."—Zig Ziglar.

SOURCES OF LEARNING

Continue to read/listen to more books, attend/download seminars and engage in conversations about sales. You may pick up dozens of books of which you do not agree with 100% of the content; however, there may be one or two things you learn which could improve your results. Being a passionate learner and thinker in sales, I have never read a sales book that suits me entirely—yet, by the same token, I have never regretted reading any of them. Each one shares a new perspective and stems from another set of experiences, which matures my thinking. Keep reading.

The people around us also serve as a great source of knowledge; whether they have experience in sales, are new to the game or share a customer's point of view, each is valuable to expanding your thinking. Don't be afraid to learn from new recruits in sales. A fresh perspective can be just what you need to break long-lasting habits. As Anthony Robbins once shared, our lives are a direct reflection of the expectations of our peer group. Surround yourself with people who expect more of you and who will give you space to grow.

Find a mentor who can challenge you and teach you—someone who role-models the behaviours that you want. Your mentor does not necessarily have to be someone who is more senior than you or someone whom you secretly want to network with to get a promotion. This is a short-term way of thinking. Find a mentor who has strengths where you have weaknesses. One of my mentors is a friend who is incredibly methodical and structured in his way of thinking. He has formulas and strategies, from the way he makes big life decisions to the way he chooses which restaurants to eat at. I do not want to be exactly like him; however, I admire those qualities and have learnt the methods behind his success, and now have those qualities too.

When choosing a mentor, you don't just want someone who is good at what they do. Make sure they know the methods and the principles behind what they do so you can not only emulate their behaviours but create your own version of them—this approach is more sustainable.

Remember that great salespeople can draw on more resources than sales literature. Read books on psychology, neuro-linguistic programming, behavioural economics, leadership and more. Become a people-watcher and observe how people speak and the way they interact—this will strengthen your own self-awareness as you observe other people's bad habits. Become passionate about why people do things and how the brain works.

Become a master of conversations and you will unlock the secrets of sales.

ACKNOWLEDGEMENTS

Writing a book is not easy and not something that one can accomplish alone.

I firstly need to acknowledge my first sales trainer and now one of my closest friends, Tristan Robinson. Tristan taught me how to sell when I was a young, overly confident university student. Tristan pushed me to do things that I never imagined possible. There is still so much to learn from you.

Anthony Magro, a long-term colleague and friend, must also be acknowledged for loading me with hours and hours of research, seminar material, books and TED Talks! Without your generosity, *I Am Not a Salesperson* would be a limited view of the sales world.

Faya Hayati, childhood friend and part-time genius, also deserves an acknowledgement. With his busy lifestyle, he is always there as a sounding board and never afraid to challenge me to think differently. Your limitless wisdom inspires me to push forward and reach new heights.

I must also thank my best friend, life companion and the love of my life; my wife Anisa Vasli. Thank you for being my rock and biggest supporter. You have always believed in my crazy ideas and helped me bring them alive.

Finally, I must thank all of the people who told me that they were not salespeople and who have succeeded in sales. You inspired me to write this book. Thank you!

ABOUT THE AUTHOR

Sana Vasli has spent his career working in sales, sales management, learning & development, consulting and sales transformation. He has worked with organisations in a variety of industries from subscription television to financial services.

Where he goes sales go up and people stay happy—evident from the content within this book.

Sana co-founded an innovative iPhone and Android app teetor, which connects mentees and mentors together. Follow Sana on LinkedIn to stay in touch.

Made in the USA
Middletown, DE
07 October 2015